KT-467-644

The Research Project

How to write it

Fifth Edition

Ralph Berry

Routledge
Taylor & Francis Group

LONDON AND NEW YORK

CORK CITY LIBRARY	
05334221	
LBC	09/02/2006
	£12.99

First published 1966 as *How to Write a Research Paper*
by Pergamon Press

Second edition published 1986
by Routledge
Third edition 1994, reprinted 1995 (twice), 1996
Fourth edition 2000, reprinted 2001
Fifth edition published 2004
by Routledge
2 Park Square, Milton Park, Abingdon, Oxon OX14 4RN

Simultaneously published in the USA and Canada
by Routledge
270 Madison Avenue, New York, NY 10016

Routledge is an imprint of the Taylor & Francis Group

© 2004 Ralph Berry
Chapter on *Using the Internet for Research* © 2004 Robert Eaglestone

Typeset in Sabon and Goudy by
Florence Production Ltd, Stoodleigh, Devon
Printed and bound in Great Britain by
TJ International Ltd, Padstow, Cornwall

All rights reserved. No part of this book may be reprinted or
reproduced or utilised in any form or by any electronic,
mechanical, or other means, now known or hereafter invented,
including photocopying and recording, or in any information
storage or retrieval system, without permission in writing from
the publishers.

British Library Cataloguing in Publication Data
A catalogue record for this book is available from the British Library

Library of Congress Cataloging in Publication Data
A catalog record for this book has been requested

ISBN 0–415–33444–6 (hbk)
ISBN 0–415–33445–4 (pbk)

The Research Project

Cork City Library
WITHDRAWN FROM STOCK

N   )n, this guide to project work continues to
b   source for all students undertaking research.
               right through from preliminary stages to
cc   *arch Project: How to write it* sets out in clear
ar   e main tasks involved in doing a research
pr

-
-              y effectively
-
-              composing the project
-              otnotes, documentation and a bibliography
-              mmon pitfalls.

F   throughout, this new edition features a chapter on
m   ost out of the Internet, from knowing where to start
to   g the quality of the material found there.
·   eatures include a model example of a well-researched,
cle   written paper with notes and bibliography and a chapter
on getting published in a learned journal for more advanced
researchers. Whether students are starting out or experienced in
research, *The Research Project: How to write it* is an essential tool
for success.

Ralph Berry has taught at universities around the world, including
the University of Malaya, the University of Ottawa, the University
of Massachusetts, LaTrobe University (Melbourne), the University of Canterbury (New Zealand) and Kasetsart University in
Bangkok, Thailand. He is the author of numerous scholarly books
and articles.

'This book has long been a recommendation of mine for students engaged in research, and the new material by Robert Eaglestone on 'Using the Internet for research' makes it more comprehensive than ever. The Internet can be a huge benefit for many researchers but those starting out on a project require help to discriminate the quality of online resources. *The Research Project* provides clear and practical advice on how to make best use of valuable material while avoiding the junk.'

Jason Whittaker, author of *The Internet: The Basics* and *The Cyberspace Handbook*

'A concise manual, providing indispensable guidance to students at all levels in a straightforward and readable form.'

Jamal Ardehali, *Glasgow University*

'Brilliantly clear dos and don'ts of doing research.'

Barbara Senior, *University College Northampton*

'This is a much needed book. I shall recommend it to all students that I teach, both undergraduate and postgraduate. It's clearly laid out, approachable and should prove invaluable.'

Julian Petley, *Department of Human Sciences, Brunel University*

'A clear, no fuss, no frills practical guide.'

H. Dyer, *School of Education, University of Gloucestershire*

Contents

Preface to the Fifth Edition

I have thought carefully about what needs changing for this edition, and what should stand. The biggest change since the first edition has been in knowledge gathering. When I wrote the first edition, paper copy was everything. There were no electronic resources. It had to be published or unpublished paper resources that we considered, with a glance towards oral history and artefacts. The position has now totally changed. The Internet has revolutionized research at the highest level and, even more, at the student level. I have addressed this by adding a chapter by a specialist on using the Internet for research. But I have not excluded what I wrote for the Fourth Edition, since I feel some students may need more elementary information and may appreciate the hands-on approach which has always been a feature of *The Research Project*. There may be some slight repetition between the original book, now revised and updated, and this new chapter but I cannot believe this will be a problem. This is not a book to be read cover to cover, but rather one to be consulted. The student will take from it whatever is appropriate to the task in hand.

Most importantly the sections on writing the paper are vital. Recent reports from universities have shown that the tick-box approach of much of today's education ill equips students for a task requiring a sustained effort to think and write logically. That is where Chapters 5, 6 and 8 have particular value. Chapter 7, the Specimen Paper, although print-based and written some time ago, has been retained because it shows what is needed in terms of scholarly disciplines and the ability to write lucidly and logically. A foreword to it gives some indication how today's electronic resources could have been used effectively.

Introduction

This guide is intended as an introduction to the research paper. It is designed to be relevant to students at all levels of higher education. The techniques discussed are such as must be employed in even the simplest research assignment, and in the more demanding tasks that students may have to face later in their careers.

The terms of reference of an assignment may vary widely. It may be called a research paper, a thesis or even a dissertation. Its objective may be a neutral compilation of fact, or the achievement of original conclusions. Its length may range from 2000 to upwards of 10,000 words. But the central situation remains unchanged: the writer will be expected to demonstrate a mastery of the scholarly disciplines. These may be defined as the ability to draw on a reasonably wide range of recognized authorities; to learn something of the techniques of getting the most out of a library system; to sustain the labour of taking accurate notes over a long period; to digest them into a shapely and lucid whole; and to present them with due respect for the acknowledged conventions of documentation. At all levels these remain the major concerns of the researcher.

The acquisition of these scholarly skills is, for American first-year college students, the subject of a specific course, usually lasting half a session. The course is a formal requirement and is backed by a wide selection of excellent manuals. British students, by contrast, are most unlikely to receive more than a little token instruction, but rather are expected to pick it up as they go along. The American manuals, some of which may be available to them, are not always relevant to the British educational system, or to the resources available to British students. Yet the preparation of a research paper (let us say, in practice, a paper that goes distinctly beyond the limits of a normal essay) is increasingly a feature of the student scene here, as it has long been in the United States. My aim in writing this guide is to provide the necessary guidance in a straightforward and readable form.

In writing it, I have made certain assumptions that I should now make clear.

1   I am not concerned with basic composition, and have no intention of telling my readers how to write sentences. The development of a coherent argument, however, is, I feel, so much a part of the research paper that I discuss it in Chapters 5 and 6. But otherwise I assume that my readers will turn to manuals of English composition for any guidance that they may need in that field.

2   I assume that the researcher needs, not simply a series of imperatives and recommendations, but the reasons for the recommendations. Working by rote can never lead to first-class research. Accordingly, I have tried, as far as seemed feasible, to justify the advice I give; and to consider the perfectly reasonable objections that a student might well make, if present to discuss the point with me.

3   Next, I am not concerned with purely scientific and technical areas of research. These require a specialized and formal type of report, which is outside the scope of this manual.

4   This guide was conceived as an introduction to the research paper; and I have sometimes been in some doubt as to what should be left to common sense. At the risk of rightly offending some of my readers, I have on occasion included material that might well have been left unwritten. For example, it sounds banal to advise readers to keep a photocopy, or backup disk, of their work. I know and I apologize. But I have known students to whom the advice would have been useful.* I do not see why experience has to be, as Bismarck termed it, 'the name we give to our mistakes'. It can be passed on. I have applied

---

* We all need to learn at some point. The distinguished historian A. J. P. Taylor writes of himself: 'I received no instruction how to conduct research. I was not even warned to put down the number of the document I was copying, which caused me a great deal of unnecessary work later.' A. J. P. Taylor, 'Accident Prone or What Happened Next', *Encounter*, Vol. 49 (October 1977), pp. 53–61 (p. 54).

one simple test on issues of superfluous advice. I have asked myself: 'Would it have been useful to me, as a student?' If the answer is yes, in it goes.

5 Finally, I assume that all papers will be presented in typescript or word-processed format. This is now widely recognized as the only acceptable medium for presenting a paper, but I wish to draw attention to its symbolic importance. Handwriting belongs to the sphere of personal communication. To the argument that handwriting 'shows character', the short answer is that character should be revealed, if at all, by the choice of words, not the style of handwriting. Absence of handwriting implies the acceptance of an impersonal code of conventions. The conventions and techniques embodied in a research paper will be of general and enduring value, beyond the college level. The sort of person to whom all reports are submitted – research supervisor, chief executive, editor – is interested primarily in the content, presented in a frictionless medium. An accepted format admits implicitly this situation.

The matter of format reveals in part the whole philosophy for the research paper. The keywords in this philosophy are organization, discipline and convention. These words may not be wholly welcome to all my readers, and I should perhaps offer a gloss on them. For most students, the English essay will have been strongly associated in the past with imagination, creativity, self-expression and a somewhat loose approach to form. These are perfectly proper concepts, which have an excellent educational justification. I merely point out that they are irrelevant here. Yet, in my experience, students tend to carry over into the realm of the research paper attitudes and aims, formed in the field of creative writing, that have no place in research. The kind of writing for which this guide is designed, on the contrary, is concerned with the critical assessment of existing authorities. The philosophy, then, can be defended thus. Organization is necessary for the efficient allocation of one's time and effort, and for the presentation of a paper whose internal structure is balanced and sound, and whose argument proceeds along logical lines. Discipline is central to the long labour of sifting authorities, and adding one's own critical comments only when these authorities have been fully assimilated. Conventions are vital in a context where one writes not for oneself, but for a critical public – a public whose face may change (professor, departmental head, director) but whose standards remain approximately the same. The student will address the paper to such people, and ultimately may join them. And this is the true justification of conventions, that they offer freedom of movement within a larger group. Students need not fear that these tedious conventions are cramping: ultimately they will serve to free the power of expression.

Chapter 1

The choice of subject: using the library

In this and the following chapters I intend to consider the problems of the research paper in the order in which they present themselves to the student. The first – and, to my mind, by far the greatest – problem is the choice of subject and, more particularly, of title. The general area of study is hardly a problem. A field of study, such as the 1914–18 poets, or trade unions, or the psychology of aesthetics, is selected or assigned. Three thousand words, say, have to be written on a topic in which the student is presumably interested. But at this stage the student is nowhere near fixing a *title* for the paper. It is clear that 'Trade Unions', for example, is unacceptable as a title. It is far too broad. The topic will have to be defined and limited after some preliminary reading, preferably in consultation with the student's supervisor. Even then the title may well have to remain provisional. Suppose one originally started with the vague idea of 'Trade Unions', and, after some preliminary reading, reduced it by stages to 'Trade Union Attitudes in the 1990s'. Even this might, on further reading, prove to be too broad a topic to handle adequately within the limits of the paper. One might well finish up with 'Trade Union Attitudes to the Euro'. The subject is becoming more focused and does promise to deliver some specific goods.

Here, then, is perhaps the first lesson of research; it can, in a very general way, be planned, but not blueprinted. One simply does not know what one is going to discover. These discoveries may lead to a complete change of direction. So be it: but at least this possibility should be taken into account in the planning stage. It is, then, desirable to limit one's topic *as soon as possible* to eliminate wasteful and unproductive reading; but one has to keep the title provisional as long as possible. The sheer pressure of notes and ideas has a way of imposing its own limitations, or even indicating its own path. The student's own developing interest in one area of the subject may also be a vital factor.

Then again, the formal objective of the paper has to be clarified at once. There is, strictly, a distinction between a *report*, which simply relates facts in neutral fashion, and a *thesis*, which definitely seeks to draw conclusions and assert an evaluation of the material. In practice this distinction tends to be blurred. Unless otherwise stated in the terms of reference, there is no reason why the student should not draw conclusions from the material studied. The whole matter of purpose, however, is one to be taken up with the supervisor at the beginning of the assignment. Since this purpose will inform and limit the labour of several weeks or months, its importance needs no emphasizing. I recommend a thorough discussion of the purpose with the student's supervisor, at the very beginning of the assignment.

The process, then, is one of restriction. A field is narrowed down to a title, which itself states or implies the objective of the research. One further factor has to be considered before the final decision on the title has hardened. It is useless to embark on a project before satisfying oneself that an adequate range of sources is at hand. The value of any work of research depends almost entirely on the sources used, a thought one might well bear in mind before starting on a fascinating but, as yet, little-documented field like, say, 'The Search for Weapons of Mass Destruction in Iraq'. Even with less immediate topics, one has to ask a few brutally realistic questions. Have the books (or papers) actually been written on the subject? If so, are they available in the college library? Can I pursue the enquiry through another library, perhaps via Inter-Library Loan, or through the Internet?

Clearly, the whole issue of choosing a subject makes little sense until it is related to the available sources. The chief source-gathering area is normally the college library. So far, I have treated the issue on the theoretical plane, but in fact it will be determined by the practical situation. It is high time to consider the practice of the matter.

Using the library

The student's first task will be to become fully acquainted with the resources of the college or university library. The logical place to start is with the library staff and the information they can provide.

The library staff

Making the acquaintance of the library staff is a high priority for any researcher. They know all about the facilities of the library and it is folly to neglect the personal channels to the sources. They can usually supply printed or duplicated handout material, offering a useful guide to the library's layout and particular features. This will include important information on special collections, which may be separately housed and catalogued. It will also give information on the particular methods used for cataloguing in the library, and on such matters as CD-ROMs, microform materials, thesis abstracts, photocopying facilities, availability of computers and computer databases, or access to the Internet. The library may have specialist librarians who can offer assistance with specific subject areas, with bibliographic work and with information services. They will also have information on the IT services available and the courses or training provided to make full use of them. Increasingly libraries are becoming much more than collections of books and, to obtain the fullest benefit from them, the student should not hesitate to consult the library staff. I have invariably found librarians to be courteous and helpful, indeed most anxious that their library should be efficiently used. The librarian is the expert and the expert should be consulted.

The open shelves

Contact having been made with the librarian, students may feel that the obvious place to begin research is the open shelves. Certainly a familiarity with their layout is essential. There are two principal classifications: the Dewey Decimal System and the Library of Congress Classification.

(a) *The Dewey Decimal System* classifies books according to the following broad scheme:

000–099	General Works
100–199	Philosophy and Psychology
200–299	Religion

300–399	Social Sciences
400–499	Languages
500–599	Pure Sciences
600–699	Technology: Applied Sciences
700–799	Fine Arts and Recreation
800–899	Literature
900–999	General Geography, History and Travel
F	Fiction in English

These broad categories are further subdivided. For example, Literature is divided thus:

800	Literature
810	American Literature
820	English Literature
830	German Literature
840	French Literature
850	Italian Literature
860	Spanish Literature
870	Latin Literature
880	Greek Literature
890	Minor Literatures

These categories are then further broken down. English Literature, for example, is redivided thus:

821	Poetry
822	Drama
823	Fiction
824	Essays
825	Oratory
826	Letters
827	Satire and Humour
828	Miscellany
829	Anglo-Saxon Literature

Each of these broad groups is then further divided by the use of three decimal places, to give ever more gradations of subject matter. To find the exact placement of a book on the shelves quickly, students may also find it helpful to know the practice of many large libraries of assigning a book an additional author classification. The book *Graven Images* by Allen I. Ludwig, for example, has the Dewey Decimal number 718 and the additional author number L966g. Fairly obviously, this is derived from the first letter of the author's surname, plus various numbers standing for other letters of the alphabet.

(b) *The Library of Congress Classification* has the large groupings of subjects lettered as follows:

A	General Works – Polygraphy
B	Philosophy – Religion
C	History – Auxiliary Sciences
D	History and Topography (except America)
E–F	America
G	Geography – Anthropology
H	Social Sciences – Sociology
J	Political Sciences
K	Law
L	Education
M	Music
N	Fine Arts
P	Language and Literature
Q	Science
R	Medicine
S	Agriculture – Plant and Animal Industry
T	Technology
U	Military Science
V	Naval Science
Z	Bibliography and Library Science

Within these large groupings, further letters and numbers give the subdivisions. I select one group to show how this is done.

N   Fine Arts
N   General
         8700–9084

NA   Architecture
         4600–6113 Religious architecture.
         7100–7625 Domestic architecture.

NB   Sculpture and related arts

NC   Graphic Arts in general. Drawing and design.
      Illustration.
          1300–1765 Caricature. Pictorial humour and satire.

ND   Painting
          1700–2399 Water-colour painting.
          2890–3416 Illuminating of manuscripts and books.

NE   Engraving. Prints
          1000–1325 Wood engraving. Xylography.
                      Japanese prints.
          1400–1775 Metal engraving. Colour prints.
          1940–2225 Etching. Dry point.
          2250–2539 Lithography.

NK   Art applied to industry. Decoration and ornament.
          1700–3505 Interior decoration. Home decoration.
          3700–4695 Ceramics. Pottery.
          5000–6050 Enamel. Glass. Stained glass. Glyptic
                      arts.

This is one example. Further information for other groups and for further subdivisions within this group may be found in *Outline of the Library of Congress Classification*.

Familiarity with these methods of placing books will enable students to go straight to what seems the most relevant section for their purpose. But to begin a research project here, at the open shelves, is inadequate and may prove misleading. Certain books may be out on loan; others may be held in stock in the basement. Then again, the physical grouping of books on a shelf may not correspond to the complexities of the subject. Even a simple case will demonstrate the point. Suppose one were writing a paper on the Greek civilization of the Classical era. One might start looking at the Ancient History shelves, and discover certain relevant volumes there. But an important work like Ehrenberg's *The Greek State* might be shelved under Political Science; Richter's *Greek Sculptors and Sculpture* under Fine Arts; and Kitto's *Greek Tragedy* under Literature. It is clearly impossible to take in all the books relevant to a theme, scattered as they are around the library, merely by looking at the open shelves. The only way to make sense of the situation is by going back to the catalogue.

The catalogue

The catalogue is the logical place to begin one's research. It is a register of all the books in the library. There are different methods of cataloguing the books, and students will need to spend a little time familiarizing themselves with the one used by their own library.

A common method is to classify each book by author, title and subject. There are, however, several cards in the index for each book: that which identifies a book by the author's name; that which lists it under its title; and those which list it under one or more subject headings (such as Italian Renaissance or Shakespeare). In each case the information is entered on a 5 × 3 in. card (see Figure 1).

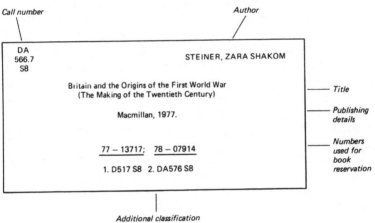

Figure 1. Card index card.

From the researcher's point of view, there are three items of primary importance on this card: the author, title and call number. To these may be added the date of publication, an important factor in assessing the worth of the book. The cards for each entry of the book are identical, except that those which list it under its title or subject have this additional heading typed above the author's name.

The subject cards are of obvious value to the researcher. If one is beginning an investigation from the start – that is, with little to go on but the subject approach – one has to use a little ingenuity, and not be put off by drawing a few blanks. Thus Socialist Party may yield nothing, but Political Parties will. It is as well to remember that the cross-referencing in the library may not be perfect, and it is always worthwhile to try under several subject headings. Thus I would investigate Machiavelli under Machiavelli; Italian Literature; Italian Renaissance; Italian History; Political Science. One might turn up several cards not duplicated under other subject headings. The more complex a subject, the more likely one is to need various and ingenious assaults upon the card index. One may obtain some idea of how various book titles may be listed under subjects, by taking a few examples where one knows the author and title, and looking up the card index to see what alternative listings they appear under.

But perhaps this method is not the one used. The card index may list only author and title and there may be additional methods to track down the books by subject. One such method, of great help to the researcher, is to have a separate small subject catalogue, which, instead of listing specific titles, gives the number classification under which to look in a separate classified catalogue. This classified catalogue lists all books in numerical/ alphabetical order of their Dewey Decimal/Library of Congress classification. Having determined the relevant number of one's own subject interest, it is as easy to check the titles under that classification as to run one's eye along the shelves. The big difference is that in the classified catalogue they are all there, whereas on the shelves many are missing, because they have been borrowed or are shelved elsewhere. The classified catalogue has further advantages. One can see at a glance such important details as publication date without actually handling the volume. Moreover, the classified catalogue has a cross-referencing facility to books which, because their subject matter may have other relevancies, have been shelved under another classification. An example will make this clear. For the specimen paper on Nazi Propaganda, the student went first to the Subject Index for National Socialist Party: Germany: History, and was thus directed to the Classified Catalogue DD253.2–253.8. (This particular library used the Library of Congress Classification.) Under these numbers a variety of relevant titles emerged, but so did others; for example, Film Propaganda, classified as DK226.3, and Propaganda and the German Cinema, classified as PN3266.5. Each of these works was listed under the original classification number in square brackets. The usefulness of this classified system for obtaining a clear view of all relevant books held by that particular library, wherever shelved, needs no labouring.

As stocks of books increase and space becomes more limited, libraries increasingly turn to new forms of technology. One such method is the use of microforms. Some record all recent acquisitions on microfiches; others have transferred their whole catalogue to microfiches, or are in process of doing so. Since each microfiche can hold a very large number of titles, there is an obvious saving of space for the library. For the library users also, once they have mastered the techniques of scanning the microfiche, there is a great saving of effort.

The microfiches are contained in a binder, and each covers a portion of the alphabet, for the combined author and title catalogue, or a portion of the Numerical/Alphabetical classification, for the Classified Catalogue. The entry for each book contains essentially the same information as the card, but reduced to a very tiny form, which can be brought up to full size by the microfiche reader. To find the entry required it is necessary to place the

A1	A2	A3	A4	A5	A6	A7	A8	A9	A10	A11	A12	A13	A14	A15	A16	A17	A18
B1	B2	B3	B4	B5	B6	B7	B8	B9	B10	B11	B12	B13	B14	B15	B16	B17	B18
C1	C2	C3	C4	C5	C6	C7	C8	C9	C10	C11	C12	C13	C14	C15	C16	C17	C18
D1	D2	D3	D4	D5	D6	D7	D8	D9	D10	D11	D12	D13	D14	D15	D16	D17	D18
E1	E2	E3	E4	E5	E6	E7	E8	E9	E10	E11	E12	E13	E14	E15	E16	E17	E18
F1	F2	F3	F4	F5	F6	F7	F8	F9	F10	F11	F12	F13	F14	F15	F16	F17	F18
G1	G2	G3	G4	G5	G6	G7	G8	G9	G10	G11	G12	G13	G14	G15	G16	G17	G18
H1	H2	H3	H4	H5	H6	H7	H8	H9	H10	H11	H12	H13	H14	H15	H16	H17	H18
I1	I2	I3	I4	I5	I6	I7	I8	I9	I10	I11	I12	I13	I14	I15	I16	I17	I18
J1	J2	J3	J4	J5	J6	J7	J8	J9	J10	J11	J12	J13	J14	J15	J16	J17	J18
K1	K2	K3	K4	K5	K6	K7	K8	K9	K10	K11	K12	K13	K14	K15	K16	K17	K18
L1	L2	L3	L4	L5	L6	L7	L8	L9	L10	L11	L12	L13	L14	L15	L16	L17	L18
M1	M2	M3	M4	M5	M6	M7	M8	M9	M10	M11	M12	M13	M14	M15	M16	M17	M18
N1	N2	N3	N4	N5	N6	N7	N8	N9	N10	N11	N12	N13	N14	N15	N16	N17	N18
O1	O2	O3	O4	O5	O6	O7	O8	O9	O10	O11	O12	O13	O14	O15	O16	O17	IND
P1	P2	P3	P4	P5	P6	P7	P8	P9	P10	P11	P12	P13	P14	P15	P16	P17	IND

Index

Figure 2. Microfiche grid.

microfiche on the plate of the microfiche reader in the correct position. The machine itself will have instructions for this placing, and for switching on and focusing. With a little practice, it is quick and easy to find the entry required. The machine is equipped with a grid (as in Figure 2), each letter/number combination giving guidance as to where the particular information is located on the microfiche. By moving a pointer to the relevant square, the reader can quickly find the author or title required. The two squares on the bottom right of the grid, marked IND, should be located first, as they provide the index for location of information on that microfiche. Thus, if the author or title one wants is located at K8, one moves the pointer to that square. Once one becomes familiar with them, the microfiches will be found easier and quicker to read than a card index, especially as one can deal with a large bibliography from one location.

In many libraries both the card index and the microfiche have been superseded by the central computer database with a number of terminals. The student will find that the screen of the computer terminal gives clear instructions as to what needs to be typed in to secure the required information. One may search for a book by title, by author, by call number, by subject or by keyword. Call number or subject searches will enable one to browse through the chosen category, by typing the appropriate instructions for that particular system to move forwards or backwards. Since the system used varies from library to library, the student is advised to read carefully the leaflets provided by that particular library which explain its own system, or to follow the on-screen display. Information in the entry is shorter than that on a catalogue card, but contains all that is essential to one's purpose.

Sample computer entry

GANNON, Franklin Reid: *British Press in Germany 1936–39.* Call number: DD256.5 G278 1971.

It will be noted that the publication date is included.

As with the microfiche catalogue, the advantages of being able to carry out a rapid bibliography search from one location are obvious. The disadvantage of both systems is that at busy times there are often insufficient machines for the number of users, and each may be in use by one person for quite a long time.

In many libraries a combination of systems is used, with earlier works on a card index and later ones on computer database. Sometimes a microfiche catalogue is available as a back-up to the computer database. It is therefore advisable to be familiar with all the systems. Almost all libraries have moved to OPAC (Online Public Access Catalogue). This means that the catalogue can be accessed from outside the library via the Internet. The method of using OPAC is essentially the same as that described above for a computer database. There are clear on-screen instructions. The search may be made by title, author, keyword, subject or call number. If the search does not reveal the exact configuration typed in, one can click for related items. Clearly, if one knows the exact title or author's name, this is the best route to follow. If one does not, keyword produces better results than subject.

Some examples

Keyword BLAIR produced, amongst others:

Title	Author	Date	Classmark
The Next Ten Years: Key Issues in Blair's Britain	Rentoul, John	1996	DA591.B5

Subject TRADE UNIONS + EUROPEAN COMMUNITY produced, amongst others:

Classmark	Title	Author	Date
JE445.6.H4	*Industrial Relations and the Environment in the EC*	Hildebrandt, Eckart	1992

Author Search CLARK, ALAN produced more than one author. In this case, the dates 1928–99 enabled the correct author to be identified; without it one would have had to try them one by one. Often the year of birth (and not death) of an author is given, and this may well be enough information.

Title	Date	Classmark
The Tories: Conservatism and the Nation State 1922–1927	1998	JD232.05

When one relevant book has been identified, it is always possible to look for others on related topics through the classmark search, rather as one might do by physically looking along the shelves.

Some OPAC catalogues also allow the search to include reading lists or lists of websites as well as the categories above. In these cases the student can type in the course title and obtain such a list which has the authority of the course tutor to validate it. This is obviously extremely useful for a research project which is course related.

What is included in OPAC catalogues varies according to the particular library's policy. They may include periodicals, unpublished theses and files of press cuttings as well as books.

The catalogue, then, whatever form it takes, offers the major access to the books in the library. The investigation cannot end there, however, for two reasons. First, the catalogue refers only to books stocked in that library. Second, it will give very limited guidance to the periodical section.

The periodical section

The periodical section is, in some ways, the researcher's happy hunting ground. It is authoritative because it contains the work of specialist writers in specialist fields. It is often easier to publish a book than an article in a major journal. Then, it offers information which may be simply unavailable in book form, anywhere. It is principally a matter of time lag. A book takes a long time to write and a longer time to publish. Once published, it may retain its position of ever-diminishing authority for many years. But a reputable journal may contain fresh and important facts that are months, weeks, perhaps even days, old. No book can compare with this authority. The periodical section offers the researcher the prize of being as up-to-date on the subject as it is humanly possible to be.

How is information about these articles to be gleaned? The articles are not listed in the card index. Only the journal or newspaper would be listed, probably in a special catalogue within the periodical section. This special catalogue will guide one to the periodicals actually held by the library, current numbers of which can be investigated on the shelves.

How to get the best out of the periodical section

Visit it. Not by tapping the 'Enter' key, but by physically acquainting yourself with the contents and layout of the periodical section, in the areas that interest you. There is no other way. Suppose, say, that you want to study current theatre journals. The titles will be displayed in alphabetical order in the Humanities section. You will naturally turn to the titles beginning 'Theatre', and you will find them. *Theatre Forum, Theatre Notebook, Theatre Research International,* and *Theatre Record* should strike the eye at once. But you will need to look farther to find *New Theatre Quarterly* and *Essays in Theatre,* and you should keep an eye on *Comparative Drama.* Then you need to find out the form of each journal, and this can only be done through browsing. You will soon discover that *Theatre Survey* is largely devoted to American theatre history, *Theatre Notebook* to British theatre history, and *Theatre Record* to the latest reviews of London productions. If you are looking for *Plays and Players,* you need to know that it has ceased publication. That is what happens with many journals. Nothing beats a hands-on familiarity with the current shelves.

And theatre is a fairly limited, focused subject area. All major subject areas break out of their natural, linguistic limitations. 'Renaissance' leads you at once to *Renaissance & Reformation, Renaissance Studies* and *Renaissance Quarterly.* But then comes *Sixteenth Century Journal,* and perhaps *Seventeenth Century.* The Renaissance takes in history, culture, art and literature; so you should look for *English Literary Renaissance* and *Studies in English Literature 1500–1900: The Renaissance* (one quarterly issue in a year). A wide range of journals might publish the occasional article on the Renaissance, including *Review of English Studies, Modern Language Review* and *Modern Philology.* The latest issues of journals do not arrive with a flourish of trumpets. You just have to get into the habit of glancing at the contents page of each journal, so that you can pick up early an article that seems to bear upon your work. The open shelves of current periodicals give some idea of the astounding wealth of specialist journals.

So much for current issues of periodicals. Bound or boxed collections of past numbers will also be available, probably shelved in another part of the library, or, for reasons of space, transferred to microfilm. The library staff are always happy to explain how to use microfilm machines. Familiarity with them is becoming increasingly necessary for research. Recent annual compilations of newspapers such as *The Times* and *The Sunday Times* are also now available as CD-ROMs and these may be available in the library. And much of this material is also available on the Internet as is explained below. The library staff will be able to help with information on what is available, and how to acquire access to it.

When the journals or newspapers relevant to the topic have been discovered, however, the student is still a long way from finding the particular articles needed, and for this must turn to the Bibliography section.

The Bibliography section

The Bibliography section of the library provides students with a guide to information on their subjects more comprehensive than that readily discoverable from the catalogue. As its name implies, it is concerned with providing information about what books or articles have appeared on any given subject, whether stocked by that library or not. With the increased availability and use of CD-ROMs and the Internet, the Bibliographical section of the library is tending to shrink in its print form so that all the works mentioned here may not be available, but it should be possible to access the material electronically.

In the Bibliography section may be found works giving classi-fied lists of periodicals, such as *Ulrich's International Periodicals Directory*, the most widely used directory, which is searchable online and also produced on CD-ROM. There is also *Willings Press Guide*, which gives good coverage of British newspapers and general interest magazines. These will lead the student to relevant periodicals. Once located, they then have to be analysed. Such analysis is assisted by the fact that virtually all reputable journals publish an annual index. The major newspapers also produce comprehensive indexes. The Times group publishes an index, which includes not only *The Times*, but also *The Times Literary Supplement*, *The Times Educational Supplement* and *The Times Higher Education Supplement*. There are also indexes to *The Financial Times* and *The Guardian*. Major libraries may well have the indexes to foreign newspapers such as *The New York Times*, *Wall Street Journal* or *Le Monde*.

These indexes are of value if students know the journals in which articles on their subjects are likely to have appeared, or if they know that it will have been covered in the press. If they are merely looking to see what has been written, they will need further help. This is readily obtainable from the many publications devoted to the listing of periodical literature. These range from the general to the highly particularized and specialist. It is possible to list only some here.

The most comprehensive of the general works is *The Reader's Guide to Periodical Literature*. It calls itself 'a cumulative author subject index to periodicals of general interest published in the United States'. This gives some idea of its coverage. A list of the close to two hundred magazines for which articles are listed is printed in the front. It is published twice a month for about half the year, and otherwise monthly. It is cumulative. Students will therefore find the entries for the current year by their month, but the numbers for previous years reclassified into two-yearly volumes. Necessarily, entries are brief and use a number of abbreviations which make the book appear difficult. At the front of each volume a sample abbreviated entry is given with full explanation below. Careful reading of this will soon enable students to follow the method used. Once they have mastered *The Reader's Guide*, they have mastered the system used for many other Guides. Entries are listed alphabetically under author, subject and sometimes title.

To illustrate how the system works: if one is studying the origins of the Social Democratic Party/Alliance, one will find entries under Political Parties: Great Britain. I take one at random.

Sample entry

> Left, right and rising centre. C. Kennedy, il. *Maclean's* 94:35
> S 28 '81.

This means that an illustrated article, entitled 'Left, right and rising centre', by C. Kennedy, will be found in volume 94 of *Maclean's*, page 35, in the issue of 28 September 1981. It should be noted that a list of the abbreviations used for many journal names appears at the front of the Guide. Older works, mostly of the last century, since its coverage goes only to 1906, can be found in *Poole's Guide to Periodical Literature*.

Besides these works concerned with periodicals and wide coverage, there are many specialist subject indexes published, listing books as well as articles. Thus for English Language and Literature, students will find the *Annual Bibliography of English Language and Literature*, published by Modern Humanities Research Association. It contains books, periodical articles, theses and book reviews, listed under subject and author. The volumes are cross-referenced so that an entry for a review will include details of the original entry for the book reviewed. It is available on CD-ROM and by subscription through Literature Online (http://lion.chadwyck.co.uk).

Sample entry for the 1981 volume

HAYMAN, Ronald. *British Theatre since 1955: a reassessment*. (Bibl. 1979, 9152) Rev. by Eric Salmon in QQ (88) 137–44 (review article).

This means that the book was originally listed in the 1979 volume, item 9152, and that a review of it by Eric Salmon, as part of a review article, appears in *Queen's Quarterly*, Vol. 88, pages 137–44.

For the Social Sciences there is *Social Sciences Index*; 342 key periodicals are currently indexed. It is available online and in CD-ROM. A student of education might turn to *Education Index*, an American publication listing some British periodicals, or *British Education Index*.

It is possible to give only a few examples here, but for the special index devoted to their own subject students are advised to turn to more general bibliographic works. In this context I would mention first a work of wide coverage. This is *A World Bibliography of Bibliographies* by Theodore Besterman. The fourth and final edition came out in 1965–6, but a decennial supplement based on the same principles has been compiled for 1964–74. This will lead students to specialist works in their own fields.

Another invaluable work is *Walford's Guide to Reference Material*, which first appeared in 1959, but has been updated regularly. It is in three volumes: Volume I, Science and Technology, 1998; Volume II, Social and Historical Sciences, Philosophy and Religion, 2000; Volume III, Generalia, Language and Literature, the Arts, 2000. This work aims to provide a signpost to reference

books and bibliographies published mainly in recent years. Bibliographies are listed under each subject. I take some examples
on History from Volume II. The *Annual Bulletin of Historical
Literature*, published by the Historical Association, is listed.
Recently Published Articles produced by the American Historical
Association lists more than 15,000 references and claims to be
'the most current and comprehensive bibliography of periodical
literature about history available'. Bibliographies are also listed
by country, so for the Specimen Paper the student would have
found one for the Nazi era. Some Internet sites are also listed.
For example http://www.ihrinfo.ac.uk/welcome, the website of
History On-line, London Institute of Historical Research, has
30,000 items in its database, including books in print and journal
articles with abstracts. *Walford's Guide* is very wide in its coverage
and, where appropriate, includes short quotations from reviews
of works it cites.

Again, as with other aspects of the library, bibliographical
searches are being revolutionized by the use of CD-ROMs. These
can provide an enormous database for articles in learned journals
on a particular field, for thesis titles and thesis abstracts in Great
Britain, North America and some European countries. Libraries
with a well-equipped CD-ROM section may be able to provide a
CD-ROM listing of all books in print from UK publishers, for
example, Bookbank. The material available is constantly being
increased. In 1994 *The Times Educational Supplement* produced
Bookfind, listing and reviewing 500,000 titles. Increasingly this
kind of information is becoming available on the Internet. The
library staff, or their handout materials, will give guidance as to
what is available in their particular library, either as CD-ROM
or via the Internet, and how to access it. Many libraries now have
dedicated CD-ROM machines.

More information is available through the Internet. Many
libraries provide students with access through the Webserver to
BIDS (Bath Information and Data Services), located at Bath
University. BIDS has four citation Indexes (Arts and Humanities,
Science, Scientific and Technical Proceedings, and Social Sciences).
These Indexes give details of the contents of over 7000 journals.
Access is restricted to members of the university using a login
name and password. The librarian will be able to help with
information as to whether this service is provided and how to
access it. In many cases the journals themselves can be accessed

online, and if the library subscribes to them the contents can be downloaded.

The URL (Uniform Resource Locator – essentially the address) for the website for journals online is http://www.journalsonline. bids.ac.uk/JournalsOnline.

Using these methods the student should be able to track down the appropriate bibliography. The value of this is that relevant books and periodicals not on the library shelves can be identified. They can then be ordered from another library through the Inter-Library Loan system, or the researcher may pursue them to another library or through the Internet.

In this context it is worth noting that for every region of Britain there is a copyright library, that is, one entitled to a copy of every book published in the United Kingdom. These copyright libraries are, for England, the British Library (London), the Cambridge University Library, the Bodleian Library (Oxford); for Scotland, the National Library of Scotland (Edinburgh); for Wales, the National Library of Wales (Aberystwyth); and for Ireland, Trinity College Library (Dublin). For newspapers, other than those in their own library, students should be aware of the existence of the British Library Newspaper Library, Colindale Avenue, London. There are also many large reference libraries and specialist libraries in Britain. The *ASLIB Directory* referred to on page 37 gives information on all specialist libraries.

The contents of these libraries can be ascertained by consulting their websites. The British Library's new website (www.british-library.net) offers direct access to the library's online catalogue listing more than nine million items. It also provides links to other research libraries throughout the world, such as the Library of Congress. Another site from the British Library is www. education. bl.uk.

The bibliographical works cited above, as well as the information gained on specialist libraries, are all part of a larger axiom: that researchers should not believe that the sum of human knowledge, relevant to their investigation, is confined to what is under their noses.

The Internet

The most rapidly growing method of gathering information for a research project is the World Wide Web. When the third edition of this book came out in 1994 it was not even necessary to consider it: now it is impossible to ignore it.

In the previous section consideration was given to Internet access to library catalogues, to bibliographical indexes and to electronic journals. It is now time to turn to more direct access to information from the Internet.

It can be said now that anything can be found out from the Web. Increasingly, children in schools are being taught to access information in this way. No researcher can afford to be unaware not only of what is on offer, but also of the pitfalls as well as the advantages.

The first thing is the sheer quantity and lack of organization of the information offered. In a similar way to finding the book or article relevant to the research topic, the researcher must find the appropriate website. There are several avenues to this.

The student's supervisor may suggest appropriate websites, or if the research project is course related there may be a list of websites, parallel to a reading list, available.

Again, a relevant website may be known from other aspects of the research: the familiar printed word may lead to it. *The Times* occasionally has details of a website at the foot of a report where more information can be found. This is headed TIMESONLINE. An example is www.timesonline.co.uk/student which follows a story about universities. If no such link is given, the researcher may go to the general *Times* website www.timesonline where an index will lead to the appropriate site. *The Guardian* also in addition to its general website www.guardian.co.uk has a number of LINKS, for example www.guardian.co.uk.arts. *The Financial Times* has lists under ONLINE such as www.ft.com/media. Other newspapers also have their own sites, organized on similar lines, though without the links. Thus students will find *The Independent* under www.independent.co.uk and *The Daily Telegraph* under www.telegraph.co.uk. *The Sunday Times* in its News Review Section has a division DOORS giving various current websites. These have the advantage of being up-to-date. The web is in a constant state of flux and many sites disappear or are renamed.

Finally a good starting point is to use one of the directories of websites. While many of the listings are of a popular rather than a scholarly nature, they can act as a useful starting point for getting the feel of more general aspects of what is available and for linking to other sites.

The *Internet Rough Guide* is a useful manual which provides some sites. *The Hutchinson Directory of Web-sites* contains details of over 5000 sites classified by broad subjects. It is UK produced, which is an advantage at a time when so much of the Internet is dominated by American sites. There is also *The Internet Bible* by Brian Underdahl and Edward Willett. But, of course, the proviso above still applies: many of these sites may have disappeared.

Using one of these methods, one may be able to go directly to a website and from it establish links to other sites. Links to other documents are embedded in the text in the form of words in hypertext, shown in another colour or underlined. To follow the link, one must click on the words/words in hypertext and a new site will open up. To return to the earlier text, one must click on the back button, an arrow facing back in the left corner of the tool bar.

If an appropriate website has not been found through the means outlined above, it will be necessary to have recourse to one of the many Search Engines. The number of these is increasing all the time. Some are mentioned here to serve as examples and other popular ones are listed in an appendix at the end of the book, together with their URLs.

For an exhaustive treatment of using Search Engines I recommend accessing *The Spider's Apprentice: A Helpful Guide to Web Search Engines* (http://www.monash.com/spidap4.html).

Two methods of searching can be employed: via a directory or via a Word Search.

Searching via a directory

Most Search Engines have some kind of list of categories on their opening page. Yahoo!, one of the first Search Engines, is particularly strong on categorizing its content, passing the user from site to site in a logical sequence. To test this I pursued an archaeological interest through.

I clicked **Arts and Humanities** from the initial directory list, then **Humanities**, then **Classics**, then **Archaeology**, then **Roman**, and, from an interesting list, selected 'A Cache of Vintage Ships', a recent archaeological discovery at Pisa (website http://www. archaeology.org/9907/etc/pisa.html). Hypertext links at the end of the article enabled me to access further sites, on individual ships or on the possibility of a new museum to enshrine the discoveries.

Similarly **Arts and Humanities – Humanities – Classics – Archae-ology – Roman – Herculaneum** led to a number of interesting sites on the villa of the papyri.

Searching via a word search

This is a skill which the student can be expected to develop progressively. It can be time-wasting and frustrating. First, one needs to look at the title of the research project and think of key concepts which can be expressed by keywords. The more exact one can make this word search, the greater the likelihood of reaching relevant information quickly. The process is similar to that of refining the title of the research project, as described in Chapter 1. But one must be aware that the Search Engine will look only for these words, with no regard for the contextual ideas which relate to the student's particular search. It will thus throw up a number of sites which seem to have little relevance in the eyes of that student.

I take as an example the subject of 'Costume in Shakespeare's Plays'. We already have three keywords here: **Costume, Shake-speare** and **Plays.**

Boolean operators, used by most Search Engines, though not by Google, can be used to refine the search. Boolean **AND** means that all the terms must appear in the documents, i.e. **Costume AND Shakespeare's Plays** ought not to yield general costume sites or information about the plays. Boolean **OR** means either term and would not be useful here. Boolean **NOT** excludes certain categories. **Costume AND Shakespeare's Plays NOT USA** would exclude American sites. Enclosing a group of word in inverted commas should lead to the Search Engine treating them as a group and not returning results for individual words. *The Spider's Apprentice*, mentioned on page 24, gives much more information on Boolean operators as well as concept-based searches.

Costume and Shakespeare's Plays turned out to be a good example of the pitfalls in word-based searches. Few of the sites that were found had any relevance to my aim. Many were about Shakespeare at various theatres with no mention of costume. Some were about costume through the ages with no relevance to Plays. Some advertised Theatre Courses or sources for hiring fancy dress costumes! One or two offered Essays that students could use.

However, persistence, using several different Search Engines and refining the search in ways suggested above, finally paid off. Using Google and the words Costume Design for Shakespeare's Plays produced an interesting site with information on an 1827 Paris production of *Hamlet*, and the Juillard Journal Online with an account of costuming for *Romeo and Juliet*. 'Costume Design AND Shakespeare's Plays', using Dogpile led to the International Design Archive where costume designs could be examined by Title, Playwright, Designer and Producer. It also led to a Theatre History website with some information. Meta-Search, via Ask Jeeves, produced a useful University of Michigan site *From Head to Toe: Costumes from Shakespeare's History Plays*. Using information gained from a recent book (Michael Mullin, *Design by Motley*, Delaware, 1996), I tried entering the name of costume designer Motley and found some relevant sites though there was no information there not in the book. The perhaps equally famous designer Tanya Moiseiwitsch yielded nothing.

In a foreword to Chapter 7, the Specimen Paper, I consider what the student, if writing that paper today, might have found on **Nazi Propaganda** (page 87 below).

My experience in these and other searches suggests that students need to be resourceful and persistent to find what they want by using Search Engines. A number of articles recently have concentrated on the difficulties. Indeed, a report in *The Times** of research about the Internet revealed the problems for Search Engines when an estimated 800 million indexed pages are on the Web in 1999, as opposed to an estimated 320 million in 1997. And now in 2004 these numbers will have soared even more. The Web is still in its infancy and the position is likely to improve. Meanwhile, for any but very recent subjects students may well find the printed word easier to access.

This brings me to the real point of the Internet: immediacy. As was stated in Chapter 1, 'A book takes a long time to write and a longer time to publish.' For subjects of recent importance the Internet can provide up-to-the-minute information. Obvious cases are company statistics and business information. Equally important are current news stories. Thus for the topic suggested in

---

* Nick Nuttall, 'Tide Has Gone Out for Most Who Surf Net', *The Times*, 8 July 1999.

Chapter 1 ('The Search for Weapons of Mass Destruction in Iraq'), a large number of sites, mostly of current news stories, was easily found by typing in Weapons of Mass Destruction in Iraq. Clearly these would need to be carefully evaluated for bias. Accessing www.bbc.co.uk/panorama yielded information on a programme specifically on this subject, broadcast on 23 January 2003. A transcript of the programme and a report from Dr Kay, under the heading *The Weapons Hunter Speaks*, could be printed out.

To sum up, then, the Internet can be a valuable tool for researchers but needs to be approached with care. Its greatest value is likely to appear where the student already knows the website, where the subject is a very recent one not already documented in the printed word, or when the search can be very exactly refined.

Let us assume, then, that the student has found on the Internet material relevant to his or her research project. This may be several pages in length. Reading through all these and taking notes while on the Internet would be expensive. There are several ways to avoid this problem. The student may work off-line, may save the material to the hard drive, or – and for me this is the preferred method – may print it out. The advantages of a printout are discussed in Chapter 4 'Taking notes', below. There is a further advantage that the printout will also contain the URL for that material and the date it was accessed. Promising websites, which perhaps are not yet clear candidates for printing out, should also be recorded by clicking on **Favourites** or **Bookmarks**, depending on the Web Browser being used. They can then be easily accessed again in the future.

Chapter 2

Using the Internet for research

Robert Eaglestone

The enormous growth of the Internet, its undeniable importance and cultural and intellectual significance make it an indispensable tool for research. However, it does have drawbacks and difficulties.

While this chapter does offer some specific details of sites, there is so much material available that it could not fail to omit much which applies to many areas of research. Moreover, the speed of the development of the net means that specific references would date extremely quickly. Instead, I have concentrated on *how to use* the Internet. This chapter, then, is in two parts. The first part concentrates on how to search the net. The second looks at how to evaluate web resources.

Part One

Searching and researching

To give a full description of the Internet would be as foolish as describing a whole library book by book. What is important for research is how to use and search this resource: the trouble is that – like libraries before catalogues – it is not organized. There are basically two ways of searching the Internet.

The first, and easiest, is the Search Engine: the most famous, google.com, has created a new verb ('to google'). As ever, personal recommendation and experimentation are the best ways of finding which engine is best for you. Currently, 'copernic' at copernic.com offers a highly specific Search Engine. The trouble with Search Engines is that you often get a lot of irrelevant results: worse, much information is simply not found at all.

A better way, and one that also has useful serendipitous consequences, is to use gateways or portals. These are, basically,
selective catalogues of parts of the net. Apart from personal recommendations, your first port of call should be JISC (Jisc.ac.uk). The
Joint Information Systems Committee offers a very full and anno-
tated resource guide for all levels of research and teaching, and I
have drawn much in this section from there. It is a 'gateway of
gateways' or 'hub', and offers all sorts of information. Similarly,
the Resource Discovery Network (rdn.ac.uk) is a 'gateway of gateways'. It is well worth browsing these sites to get a feel for the
range of material available. From these huge 'catalogues' smaller
ones, with a greater disciplinary focus, can be found: Alan Liu's
Voice of the Shuttle (http://vos.ucsb.edu/) was one of the first of
these, and is still excellent, and there are others: Artefact is the
Arts and Creative Industries hub (artefact.ac.uk) and the excellent
Humbul (humbul.ac.uk) lists net resources for the humanities.

Research data

From these portals, or via search engines, it is possible to find the
bibliography, reference and research information on line. For
example, COPAC (copac.ac.uk) provides access, free of charge,
to the merged online catalogues of twenty-four of the largest
university research libraries in the UK, with the British Library
and the National Library of Scotland. You can also access, for
example, the Library of Congress, as well as smaller, more specific
libraries. Other sources, highlighted by JISC, include the ATLA
Religion Database (catalogues, articles and essays from journals
and multi-author works on religion at http://www.atla.com), the
Archives hub (archiveshub.ac.uk) which provides free access to
descriptions of archives held in UK universities and colleges, the
British Humanities Index (an international abstracting and
indexing tool for research in the humanities) and many others.

There is also a huge number of publications online, especially of texts that are out of copyright. Literature online (Lion.
chadwyck.co.uk), for example, has thousands upon thousands of
British and American literary texts online, in a full searchable
form (however, you can only access this if your library has
subscribed to it). More and more publishers offer their journals
online, too. You can search for the journal by title or go to the
publisher's website.

Finally, JISC lists data services, which are really just databases of different sorts. They include Census and government surveys, editions of texts, statistics from historical sources and other data sets. Again, it is well worth looking through these.

And, of course, there is also a huge amount of material on the net which has been created either for the net specifically, or for teaching. Bibliographies for specific subjects are available, and there are websites on particular authors, areas, countries, projects and so on. Of course, the links pages on all these sites can be very useful. There are also web-based journals, which publish material.

Some of these materials are free to access, but most – especially the more authoritative and valuable ones – must be paid for. For copies of articles, the publisher has often made a deal with universities, and there are various means of getting the article: you should check how to do this with your information service providers.

Community

All these above make up the huge, virtual super-library that is the Internet. However, in terms of research, the Internet is also a very useful tool for the creation of research communities. No scholar is, or has ever really been, a lone scholar. We all stand on the shoulders of giants and interact with our peers. No small part of research is being aware of what is 'going on'. Moreover, scholarship has always been international (think of scholars going from place to place in the Middle Ages). The web has made this aspect of research much easier.

In a more commercial vein, many publishers and journals maintain lists, and will email you when articles or books in your field come out, and it is worth subscribing to a few of these.

There are also discussion lists, where issues and debates are aired by contributors from all over the world. Some of these are very well organized, and provide book reviews, specialized forums, interviews with major figures and so on. In order to have a sense of what is going on, it can be important to be involved with these. Indeed, some also have archives of past discussions that can be very useful: many articles cite such discussions as starting points for developing their ideas. Two caveats, however. First, you may receive far too many email messages, which is frustrating, so you may need to moderate your involvement. Second, of course, these lists can host very heated discussions, which are time-consuming and can easily become very personal.

It is also important to find out where your discipline's main 'calls for papers' sites are. These vary from subject to subject, and usually there are three or four places. However, it is always worth visiting or subscribing to these, as they can provide useful sites indicating where best to disseminate your research. Likewise, most major conferences now host a website with information, and sometimes they have the papers online too.

Part Two

Despite all these advantages – easy access to research and bibliographic resources, the bringing together of a genuinely world-wide community of scholarship and debate – there are very significant drawbacks to using the net: the quality of information is very, very variable and can often fall well below the academic standard necessary for research.

As I have suggested, the Internet is the same as a library. Just as there are good and bad books in a library, there are good and bad sites on the Internet. But there is a key difference: even the less useful books in a library have been through a process of vetting (by editors, for example) whereas the Internet has no 'quality control' at all. This means that the bad sites really are very bad indeed. For example, a search on the name 'Toni Morrison' is as likely to turn up a terrible essay by a first-year student which they have added to their webpage as it is to uncover a really useful recent interview with the writer, put on to the net by the *Washington Post*.

There are ways to mitigate this lack of 'quality control'. Some sites – for example, the portals listed above – have editors, or moderators. Some are specifically constructed for academic use like *Fontes Anglo-Saxonici: A Register of Written Sources Used by Authors in Anglo-Saxon England* at http://fontes.english. ox. ac.uk/. Other sites are more like course packs, made up of specifically chosen excerpts from books which are referenced on the site.

It is also crucial that you evaluate any website you plan to use for academic work yourself. All the traditional tools of evaluation apply, of course. Does the text name the sources it cites?

Does the argument actually make sense? Do the spelling, grammar and composition follow normal conventions? Are there lots of typographical errors? Just as with a book from a library, these are all things that should alert a reader to the usefulness of a site.

Sonja Cameron argues that, in addition, the 'keystones of website appraisal can be said to be: Accuracy, Authority, Objectivity and Currency'. To this I would add the idea of 'audience'.

Accuracy

Of course, if you have some prior knowledge of the field, you will be in a good position to judge the level of accuracy of a site. However, often you may come unprepared to a site and then it is important to ask the following questions.

- Who wrote the site? Can they be contacted?
- Is the site edited, or (as with the portals above) has it been selected by a reputable authority as being of value?
- Do the stated aims and objectives match the actual content of the site?

Authority

One of the great benefits of the Web is the ability to make ideas public without the dulling hand of an institution, publisher and so on, and this is to be praised. Moreover, of course, someone may know a great deal and have valid things to say without having formal qualifications. However, the net is also an open door for all sorts of nonsense to appear, and one way of checking on this is knowing about the author. This may help you judge the site and its context more fully: a professor of Spanish history will – usually – know more than a sixteen-year-old student who puts an essay on Philip II up on a school site. Many webpage creators include the email address and link to their home page, especially if they are academics: it is usually worth checking these.

The hosts, too, are important. A code for an educational site (.ac.uk or .edu) indicates that a site is of respectable quality, as are .gov sites. While sites from other organizations are worthwhile, it is worth knowing that many will host pages from anybody. Advertising and pop-ups are usually a bad sign.

Objectivity

Again, this is a traditional intellectual tool for evaluating the suitability of work for research. The questions you should ask yourself are as follows. Does the site make a special case? Is there an openly stated bias? With websites, it is often simply the level of rhetoric that will make clear any bias.

Currency

The newness of the web means that things age much more quickly. This may or may not matter for some research but generally being up-to-date is a good thing. Most sites have a date which tells you when they were last updated or created. The links, too, reveal this: if they do not work, or have passed on, the site is getting old.

Audience

This is perhaps the most important criterion. Who has the site been prepared for? A site that is aimed at American high school students is not necessarily the best for European PhD students; a site set up by a media company to accompany a TV series will lack the level of detail necessary for much research. Pay attention to who is being addressed, and to the level of detail.

Of course, the format here is very revealing. Odd fonts, lots of animation, things that make the text hard to read and adverts are all signs that the page may not be the best for research use.

Finally, as Sonja Cameron writes:

> there is one crucial question left: Should you be here at all? What kind of information are you looking for, and do you think the web is really likely to provide it? Would you find your information more quickly and reliably elsewhere – in the library, for example, or in a reference work? The web is a useful repository of resources, but depending on your subject, it may have less to offer than traditional resource collections. For some subjects, the intense scrutiny of a short text may reveal more, for example, or there simply may be too much detail to take in on a website.

These subjects are covered in more detail in the following places:

- by Sonja Cameron at http://hca.ltsn.ac.uk/resources/Briefing_ Papers/bp.php?who=bp2
- by Susan E. Beck at http://lib.nmsu.edu/instruction/evalcrit. html
- by Esther Grassian at http://www.library.ucla.edu/libraries/ college/help/critical/index.htm
- by the Internet Detective at http://www.sosig.ac.uk/desire/ internet-detective.html.

Your use of the net should always bear these 'quality control' issues in mind.

The other main risk of the net, which is unlikely to trouble researchers but about which they need to be aware, is plagiarism. This serious problem has been made much worse by the net. Many universities employ 'net police' to ensure that students are not taking material from the net, and colleges and academics have access to advanced Search Engines, developed for professional use.

Different disciplines have different rules for citing the Web, and no overall policy has yet been agreed. It is usually important to cite the website, and the particular webpage with the full URL address, and to give the date on which the page was accessed.

Chapter 3

Preparing a bibliography

The first objective of the researcher is the preparation of as full a preliminary bibliography as practicable. The range of this bibliography will to some extent be determined by the requirements of the particular research paper. The types of research paper the student will be called upon to write will have a wide range. At one end of the scale a student's first assignment in this field may be a term paper, which is in essence no more than an extended essay relying on the two or three books which the library has available on the topic. At the other end may be a more ambitious venture that can fairly claim to be regarded as a minor contribution to original scholarship. Equally, students in specialized fields will concentrate their attention more particularly on some of the sources I have to consider, e.g. the Art students with visual material. To ensure that the needs of all these students are covered, I have given consideration here to all possible sources of information for even the most ambitious research project. Since I feel that even if one does not pursue the research programme with the utmost rigour, it is essential to know that it exists, I have in this chapter concentrated on the diversity and challenge of the research problem. Students whose assignments are more limited should not take fright at this, but, with the aid of their instructors, select the more readily available sources of information which will serve their needs.

To begin with, the distinction must be made between *primary* and *secondary* sources. Primary materials are first-hand accounts, reflections and statements. They are not based on other written works. They are in their original form, without having been arranged or interpreted by anyone else. Official documents, diaries and letters are the best examples of primary sources; but, generally, any sources which can be regarded as the researcher's raw material are primary. Secondary sources – by far the larger group – discuss primary sources. They consist of works which select, edit and interpret this raw material. A thoroughly integrated and well-grounded paper should draw if possible on both types of source. A historian is required to study, let us say, the letters of the Venetian Ambassador in conjunction with a general dissertation on Renaissance diplomacy. Students of art and literature must acquaint themselves with the basic products of the artist and writer before going on to consider the discussions conducted by the appropriate critics. Even students of Dewey's educational theories must occasionally plunge into the thicket of Dewey's prose. All this is obvious enough; but even the most experienced scholars sometimes fall into the pitfall of considering what Professor X said about Z – to the exclusion of what Z actually said. However learned and brilliant the discussion by subsequent authorities, one must maintain contact with the material they are discussing. Apart from the need to draw some conclusions of one's own, it is here in the primary sources that little nuggets of information may be found that have been overlooked by other researchers, for one reason or another. It is such nuggets that may give distinction to one's own work.

Bearing in mind this distinction, between primary and secondary sources, the student must first make out a list of all the available sources that may bear upon the chosen field of study. The process of evaluation, selection, reading and note-taking will come later. But this process should not be begun without a full, if rapid, survey of the sources.

These are of much greater diversity than is often realized, or exploited. The obvious sources, books and journals, I have already discussed in Chapter 1, together with the bibliographical guidance to them. But there are numerous other sources, published and unpublished, that may bear investigation.

Published sources

Many institutions issue their own printed material. The most obvious ones which spring to mind are government departments. Her Majesty's Stationery Office (HMSO) issues free about seventy sectional lists offering guidance to what is available. In their own words: 'The aim of the series of catalogues known as Sectional

Lists is to show titles of HMSO publications currently in print. Most deal with publications prepared by particular government departments.' A few of the sectional lists deal with particular subjects: for example, No. 60, *Histories of the First and Second World Wars and Peacetime Series*; or No. 69, *Overseas Affairs*.

Not all British government publications are from HMSO, however. Some departments produce their own material. Further information on this may be obtained from *British Official Publications* by J. E. Pemberton (1973), or *Official Publications* by David Butcher (1991). *The Reference Sources Handbook* ed. Peter W. Lee with Alan Day (1996) gives further information. It cites *Catalogue of British Official Publications Not Published by HMSO* (Cambridge: Chadwyck-Healey, 1980–) and *UKOP* (*Catalogue of United Kingdom Official Publications*) on CD-ROM.

Another major institution whose publications need to be considered is the United Nations. It issues the *United Nations Library Monthly Bibliography*: I. *Books, Official Documents, Serials*; II. *Selected Articles*. The Library of the United Nations Information Centre (14–15 Stratford Place, London W1) would be able to supply information on United Nations publications.

These are the most obvious sources of official publications, but many more are available. Further information on those which may be relevant to the student's own particular topic should be sought in the Bibliography section of the library. There are two especially useful guides. One is the two-volume *ASLIB Directory*. Volume I is *Information Sources in Science, Technology and Commerce*, Volume II, *Information Sources in Medicine, the Social Sciences and the Humanities*. These volumes are regularly updated. They provide a list of addresses of information sources on all manner of subjects, giving information and publications from, for example, government departments, industry and societies. The other useful bibliographical source is the three-volume *Walford's Guide to Reference Material*, already discussed in Chapter 1.

From these sources students will find what is relevant to their own subjects. Most libraries have a large stock of such material, but it will not normally be listed in the general catalogue. Students may find that in their own particular library it occupies a separate section with its own catalogue. Consultation of the library layout plan, or with the librarian, will help them track down what is already there, and the guides will show them how to procure access to what is not. The important thing is to be alive to the possibilities of the material's existence, and to explore it.

The same holds true for other material of an ephemeral nature which needs to be taken into consideration. There are, for example, current, non-indexed newspapers; catalogues to art exhibitions; press handouts, as of a candidate's speech in an election; pamphlets, news-sheets and advertisements of all kinds, including handouts from industrial firms. Again, the printed word does not account for all published sources. Records of the spoken word extend back to Tennyson and Browning; the film is not much younger; the camera came of age during the American Civil War, but for many years previously photographs had recorded the social and natural scene. To these may now be added tape recordings, for example of radio programmes, and video recordings of television programmes. The various albums, film-reels and recordings – whether restricted now to museum collection or currently available in commercial form – represent a giant supplement to the printed and published sources of the past century.

Unpublished sources

Writings which have not been made available to the general public are numerous. Diaries, letters, memoranda, rough drafts of writings published later, accounts, church registry entries, can be of enormous importance. The tendency is naturally for the most important of these records to gravitate towards the major libraries. Others remain to be sought out in the archives, national and local, all over the country; and yet more repose in private hands. Guidance as to what may be available is provided by *Guide to the Contents of the Public Record Office*, issued in three volumes by HMSO, and Sectional List No. 24, British National Archives. This is updated on micro-fiche every two years. It is also accessible by its website http://www.pro.gov.uk/finding/default. htm. There is also a National Index of Parish Registers.

Initiative allied to luck can unearth the most astonishing finds even now – and I am not referring to an exceptional field like archaeology. It is not so very long since Dr Leslie Hotson discovered, in a quite straightforward visit to the Public Record Office, the official record of the inquest on Marlowe's death by violence. More recently, Byron's official biographer found a hitherto unknown work by the poet, amongst some miscellaneous papers in the possession of his publishers, John Murray. *The Guardian*, 14 September 1999, reported the discovery at Wilton House of two unknown masques by Ben Jonson and Inigo Jones. A steady stream of less dramatic discoveries continues to reach the public; for example, the letters and diaries of those serving in the two World Wars. And this is merely the tip of the iceberg. To be sure, the relevance of such material is more obvious in the fields of literature and history than in others. But in all areas of human endeavour there is a chance that a letter, an entry in an autograph album or a draft remains behind to supplement or even modify our ideas, based on published sources, of the matter. Whether this material is in public or private hands, it is the business of researchers to bring it to light if they can.

What is true of the printed word remains true of non-printed products. The various semi-permanent forms that human activity takes – architecture, technology, art – are frequently, of their essence, unique. An example is old gravestones. But surely such remains can be photographed, and then published in book form? Certainly, but it would be naive to suppose that such publications constitute any more than a limited and often misleading selection of the material to hand, influenced as they are by fashion, chance and lack of knowledge. Art history is a good case in point. We know that Dürer was a great artist; we are only now coming to realize the greatness of Witz. The work of one has been much publicized for many years; of the other, not. The writer of one of the volumes in the Pelican History of Art* confessed that scarcely a week passed without the emergence of some previously unknown painting that caused him to modify his view. My point is this: there exists a vast corpus of relics that simply have to be seen. It is inadequate to rely on the photographed and published selection of these relics. In such situations the attribute of a good researcher approximates to that of a good reporter – leg-work.

Finally, there remain human contacts: letters or conversations. A source does not require the accolade of a permanent form to make it acceptable. There is no reason at all why a researcher should not attempt to approach a living politician, or writer, or artist, to consult him or her about some aspect. If successful, the

---

* Ellis Waterhouse, *Painting in Britain 1530–1790*. Harmondsworth, 1962, p. xv.

result may be a fascinating series of insights into matters not adequately covered by the existing sources. A short report on Sylvia Pankhurst in *The Times* elicited a letter from her son, Professor Richard Pankhurst, 7 September 1999, giving insights into her attitudes. He appended an email address which a keen researcher on the suffragettes might have followed up. It is not only the famous who can add a more immediate and personal dimension to the researcher's work. In the field of social history especially, the tape-recorded interview with someone who was personally involved can be of great value. An oral account is, in its way, every bit as valuable as a written record. If unsuccessful, then at least one will have tried. And the worst that can happen is that one will be sent away with a flea in one's ear.

The Internet offers further opportunities. It can provide unpublished theses, email contact with other researchers and chat groups.

Recording the bibliography

All these sources, published and unpublished, must be recorded before one can make a reasonable selection and whittle them down to a working bibliography. Since the details of each source used will be needed in a most exact form for footnotes and bibliography, it is necessary that extreme care should be exercised at this stage to ensure that they are full and correct. The conventional method is to write the relevant information for each source on a separate 5 × 3 in. card. In the top left-hand corner should be written the Library Call Number and, if more than one library is being used, a note as to which library the book is from. This will enable time to be saved in subsequent book location. The rest of the card should contain the bibliographical information. In addition, the student may well add a light annotation, based on a quick impression of the work (which may have been handled physically on the shelves). Thus, on a solid historical textbook published in the 1950s, one might annotate: 'Looks a readable survey – probably written too long ago for a final view – best read first.' Of some brilliant but wayward-looking piece of Shakespearian interpretation one might comment: 'Check reviews.' These quick impressions can be immensely useful later.

The point of restricting each card to one source, and one only, is that it makes the later business of discarding and rearrangement a matter of the greatest ease. The longer the work, the greater the number of sources considered, the more important it becomes to be in a position to arrange the sources alphabetically (by author) for quick consultation. Anyone who thinks this is a rather childish simplification should try the task of sorting out a list of a hundred or so titles which have simply been entered, as they come, in an ordinary notebook. It is not a labour one would wish to repeat.

The form for the bibliographical material varies according to the source itself. There is no one absolutely standardized procedure accepted by all authorities. Individual publishing houses often have their own in-house style, for example, and some universities issue their own guidelines on the presentation of theses. The student should adopt a system and maintain it consistently. The one recommended here is in conformity with the principles laid down in the *MLA Handbook for Writers of Research Papers* (Fifth edition), ed. Joseph Gibaldi (New York, 1999). For the United States the ultimate authority is the Modern Language Association of America's *The MLA Style Sheet*, and its recommendations, given in helpfully exhaustive detail and thus covering every eventuality, would also be generally acceptable in Britain.

The forms of bibliography cards for books

For all bibliography cards the author's last name is given first to facilitate the arrangement of the cards in alphabetical order for the final bibliography. The form which the information takes in the final version will be different for footnotes, from that of the final bibliography, as will be seen below (Chapter 6). The required information should be taken from the title page or, in the case of the date and edition, the next page.

Author or authors and title. Below the call number should be written the name of the author, last name first, followed by a comma, first name(s) or initials, followed by a comma; and the name of the book, underlined or italicized.

Examples

Norman, Charles, *The Muses' Darling: Christopher Marlowe.*
Lovejoy, A. O., *The Great Chain of Being.*

It should be noted that in the first title a colon had to be supplied, since publishers set out, rather than punctuate, their titles.

Where there is more than one author, the first author should be listed last name first, as for a single author, followed by a comma, and the subsequent author(s) in normal order, separated by commas.

Example

> McLuhan, Marshall, and Quentin Fiore, *The Medium Is the Message.*

If there are more than three authors, it is the practice to put *et al.* or 'and others' after the name of the first author.

Example

> Parker, Geoffrey, and others, *The Thirty Years War.*

If the work of an author is translated or edited by someone else, this additional information should be given after the author's name and the title of the work.

Example

> Castiglione, Baldesar, *The Book of the Courtier*, trans. Charles S. Singleton, ed. Edgar de N. Mayhew.

There may, however, be no author but only an editor or compiler. In this case, list the work by its title followed by a comma and the name of the editor.

Example

> *The Nazi Years: A Documentary History*, edited by Joachim Remak.

If the work is produced by a public body, list it by its title and include the other information with the publishing details.

Example

> *Case Studies in Multicultural Education: A Series of Documentary Films – Discussion Leader's Notes* (British Broadcasting Corporation, London, 1981).

The publishing details

The number of the edition used, if it is not the first, is given next in arabic numerals, e.g. 2nd edn, also any further information such as 'revised and enlarged'. Information where relevant should also be given as to the number of volumes.

The place of publication followed by a comma, followed by the date of publication, is written below the title and the edition details, if any. Figure 3 shows the layout of a complete card, giving these publishing details, and also the researcher's personal comment, on the last line. Some organizations like to have details of the actual publisher, but this is now not standard practice and is not recommended by either of the authorities cited above. Rather, the tendency is to simplify bibliographical details.

The forms of bibliography cards for articles and chapters

The cards for magazine and newspaper articles, articles from general collections, book reviews, etc., are similar to the ones for books, but the form for the titles varies, and the publication details are necessarily somewhat different.

Thus the details of the author(s), translator, etc. will be given in the same form as for a book. The title of the article, however, is enclosed in single quotation marks, and followed by a comma, even if the title ends in a question mark or exclamation mark. For a chapter in a book, the chapter title will be followed by 'in',

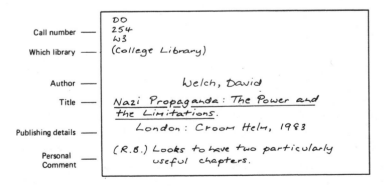

Call number —
Which library —

Author —
Title —

Publishing details —

Personal Comment —

Figure 3. Specimen bibliography card.

and the name of the book, underlined or italicized, followed by publication details, as set out above for books.

Example

> Kershaw, Ian, 'How Effective Was Nazi Propaganda?' in *Nazi Propaganda*, edited by David Welch (London, 1983), pp. 180–221.

For an article in a journal or newspaper, the title will be followed by the name of the journal or newspaper, underlined or italicized, followed by a comma and publication details. These latter are clearly different from those given for a book. What is now required is a means of identifying the particular issue. Thus, for a journal, the volume number is given, in arabic numerals, followed by the year of publication, and sometimes also the month or season, in parentheses, followed by a comma and the numbers of pages.

Example

> Arnott, Peter, 'Some Costume Conventions in Greek Tragedy', *Essays in Theatre*, Vol. 2, No. 1 (November 1983), pp. 3–18.

It should be noted that the comma comes after, not before, the parentheses. In the case of newspapers and weekly or monthly magazines, the volume number may be omitted and the complete date given, separated by commas, and not in parentheses.

Example

> Ezra, Derek, 'What Future Now for Coal?', *The Observer*, 17 February 1985, p. 10.

There may be no author for the article and, if so, this fact should be noted where possible. For example, an editorial should have the word 'editorial' in parentheses after the title and before the comma, e.g. 'New and Wrong Terms' (editorial). An anonymous review, or unsigned article, should have this fact noted in the same way.

Bibliography cards for other material

Unpublished sources should also be noted in the bibliography by whatever method is appropriate. For example, documents, unpublished theses, etc., may be identified by the author, if there is one, and location; letters and interviews by the name of the person concerned and the date; a lecture by the lecturer, the title of the lecture in quotation marks, as for the title of an article, and the place and date of delivery. A similar entry would also be made for a television or radio broadcast, except that the place of delivery would be replaced by the channel or station. Visual material should also be identified by an entry giving its exact location, as: inscription on the tomb of Lord Chief Justice Tanfield, St John Baptist Church, Burford, Oxfordshire.

Bibliography cards for Internet material

Information from the Internet is just as much copyright as information from a book or journal, and the need to cite the source is just as important. Details should be given in a form that will enable others to access the material, even though webpages change so frequently that it may be difficult. It is important for this reason to give the date the site was accessed.

Journal articles from the Internet

The recommended form is: author's surname and initials; year of publication, if given (in parentheses); title of article in single inverted commas; title of the journal, italicized or underlined; followed by 'Online' in square brackets; followed by the volume and issue number of the journal, if given. Then, as a new sentence, 'Available from:' and the website (URL) from which the material was derived. This should be followed by the date it was accessed, in square brackets.

Example

Slayman, Andrew L. (1999) 'A Cache of Vintage Ships', *Archaeology* [Online], Vol. 52, No. 4, July/August 1999. Available from: http://www.archaeology.org./9907/etc/pisa. html [accessed 18 September 1999].

Other Internet material

There are all sorts of possible sites that the student may access and discretion will be needed to record these properly. News items from the BBC would be recorded by the title [Online] and then 'Available from:', followed by the website and date accessed as above. The bibliographies for Nazi propaganda, referred to above, would be given as follows.

Example

> German Propaganda Archive, *Bibliography of English-Language Books on Nazi Propaganda* [Online], Calvin College. Available from: http://www.calvin.edu/academic/cas/gpa/mybib.htm [accessed 28 November 2003].

Evaluating the bibliography

Now comes the operation of reducing the initial bibliography to a smaller, working bibliography. I shall treat this as an entirely separate phase from the preceding one; but in practice there may be an overlap. It may take, for example, some time to elicit replies to correspondence enquiries. In the interim the student may as well get on with the job of evaluating the sources already listed. It is, however, always helpful to think of the research work as a series of orderly, planned phases. Life will contribute its own quota of disorderly, unplannable elements – there is no need to add to them unduly.

I assume, then, that everything within reason has been done to prepare a full list of sources. We now consider this bibliography. It may be quite a small one – on certain contemporary topics a working bibliography is, quite simply, all that one can find out. In such cases there is no problem. But usually the difficulty is one of restriction.

What makes a source acceptable, or more precisely, preferable? Of the infinite variety of factors that bear upon this matter, I single out two for special mention: the date of publication, and the standing of the author.

The date can very easily be weighed. It is, of course, generally true to say that the more modern a book is, the better. One can reasonably assume a second or later edition of a work to be corrected and revised. Again, the writer may be limited, but like all of us is a beneficiary of progress. Knowledge accumulates. So modernity counts; but this is much more true of some areas than others. Thus a book on nuclear submarines published in 1958 is of very limited value. One may assume it to contain an accurate view of submarines up till 1958; but so much has occurred since then that the book is bound to be outdated. In this field nothing less that the latest edition of *Jane's Fighting Ships* would suffice. On the other hand, for a thorough and well-documented history of the English Civil Wars, the historian still turns to S. R. Gardiner's *History of the Commonwealth and Protectorate*, the first volume of which was published in 1903. I suggest that one should select from the new and the old in the matter of dates. One should always have a representative of the very latest publications, and indeed aim at a preponderance of fairly recent works. But there is usually a case for including a well-written work that contains a readable epitome of the orthodox view a generation ago. What in practice one has to do is to cut out a mass of dead wood that accumulates in libraries over the years.

The standing of the author is a far more complex issue. Often one simply does not know, and cannot know. Reputation is an elusive aura. Just how good is Professor X? I can only suggest certain pointers here that the student can look for. The book may have gone through several editions. The testimony of the publisher is, to put it mildly, untrustworthy; but, if the dust-jacket refers to Professor X's 'standard' work, and the book has run through several editions, there is a fair chance that the publisher's claims may not be a league away from the truth. Somebody must have bought it. Often enough a dust-jacket (or title page) will make a biographical reference to the background and qualifications of the author, or these can be discovered from *Who's Who*, and here again readers can judge for themselves (or, possibly, draw certain inferences from the lack of satisfactory data). Favourable reviews of a previous edition may be cited on the dust-jacket. Additionally, the work may be cited in a published bibliography – for example, at the end of an article on the subject in a good encyclopedia.

All this, however, can indicate only very approximately the value of a work. The nearest approach to the truth must be obtained from the judgement of one's peers. The reviews are crucial, and ought to be studied. It is true that the same difficulties arise with the standards of reviewing, as of writing. Critics can be incompetent, biased and unfair. But a jury of sorts exists; a consensus exists.

Apart from the specialist scholarly journals, from which a considered review of a specialist work can be expected, one can look with confidence to certain newspapers and periodicals of established reputation and high standards. A forum of informed contemporary criticism is provided by, for example, *The Times*, *The Times Literary Supplement*, *The Sunday Times*, *The Observer*, *Spectator*, *New Statesman and Society* and *London Review of Books*. These are British publications, but an American publication of high repute, held by many university libraries, is *The New York Review of Books*. The list could be extended, but these provide a reliable cross-section likely to be readily available in the library.

Useful guidance to reviews is provided by certain specialist works. The most important and comprehensive of these is the *Book Review Digest*, published monthly with annual cumulation. This contains shortened reviews from selected periodicals, a list of which appears at the beginning of the guide. Usually not more than three reviews are actually quoted, but others are cited so that they may be readily found. From 1983 it is available online and on CD-ROM. Another comprehensive work is the *Book Review Index*. It is published bi-monthly, with annual cumulation, and a master cumulation for the decade 1969–79. More than 400 journals are indexed and references given to books that have been reviewed only once, as well as those reviewed more frequently. Reviews are not quoted, but the citations will readily lead the reader to the full review. From 1998 this is available online. Another more specialized work is *An Index to Book Reviews in the Humanities*. This work also cites, but does not quote, reviews from many learned journals. It should be noted that it ceased publication with the issue for 1990 and so cannot be used for more recent books.

With the aid of such works as these the student may readily track down the reviews. True, one can hardly consult them all. But one should get into the habit of checking one or two reviews, especially when a rather extreme thesis seems to be propounded.

And this leads me to my next point in this discussion of the evaluation problem. Most writers have a 'thesis' – a point of view which they seek to advance. Put more bluntly, they have an axe to grind. This is well enough; impartiality is an impossible ideal, and one does well to be sceptical of those who profess it. But it is necessary to bear in mind the author's predispositions. Is he or she an old-guard Freudian, or a revisionist, or does he or she regard psychoanalysis as finished? Is the author a Marxist, or merely left-of-centre; young or old; (on matters affecting the social activity of a given country) a native, or a foreigner? If it is practicable, one ought to set authorities at each other's throat in one's own work. The great failing in assessing one's sources is to fall under the spell of one powerfully written work. Let the opposition speak too.

There are many instances where an individual has staked a reputation or career on a particular point of view. Churchill's commitment to anti-appeasement springs immediately to mind. In his *War Memoirs* he argues powerfully and convincingly that Britain was wrong in 1938. But not even from a Churchill should a researcher accept an account uncritically. Churchill violently opposed the Munich settlement at the time; his career was intimately bound up with its consequences. He is, therefore, an immensely formidable, but highly committed advocate. So one looks to the other side for a statement of the government's case. One would anticipate, and in fact correctly, that the official biographer of Neville Chamberlain (Keith Feiling), and his later biographer (Iain Mcleod), would provide such a statement. There are naturally other later historians not passionately committed to either view. An equally controversial issue, with persuasive and committed writers, was the Suez Crisis. Here one would need to set against Anthony Eden, who argues his own case powerfully in the first volume of his memoirs (*Full Circle*), *No End of a Lesson* by Anthony Nutting, who resigned over the issue and ruined his political career. A perhaps more notorious instance of purely academic argument is A. J. P. Taylor's view of the causes of the Second World War. This has stirred up so much controversy that it has even resulted in a book, devoted to A. J. P. Taylor and his critics. The lesson to be gained from these instances is that no authority is final. None.

What is true of the printed word is even more true of the Internet. There is no yardstick such as publisher's reputation, sales or reviews to evaluate the growing mass of material on the Internet. Anyone can have a website for whatever reason: valid, such as the desire to disseminate knowledge and communicate with other scholars; dubious, such as personal vanity or desire to spread sometimes cranky ideas. It is all the more necessary therefore to evaluate the site from which the material is coming. Is it a reputable academic source, a university or college, a blue chip journal, etc., or is it an individual? If it is an individual, what can we discover about the standing of that individual? The advice given above on authors will be equally relevant here. Much Internet information comes also from what may be described as official/semi-official sources. Sites provided by reputable newspapers such as *The Times*, or by the BBC or CNN, carry the equivalent weight of these bodies. The same applies to sites provided by museums like the British Museum or the V & A, or art galleries like the National Gallery or the Tate. Information from political parties, government departments or the EU, other than of a strictly factual nature, needs to be looked at carefully for bias. Reviewing the Euro website, set up by the EU itself (http://europa.eu.int/euro), Tunku Varadarajan wrote, 'Don't expect to find a section here detailing the new currency's "cons". (After all would you find a section on atheism at the Vatican's websites?) . . . If you want plain facts, they are here, too, in abundance.'*

With the Internet a further caution is necessary: awareness of the commercial element. A publisher expects to derive money from the publication and sale of books or journals. Those who publish on the Internet must derive their income more indirectly, except in the case of academic material which is being funded, or subscribed to, by a university. The student will probably find that the material on the Internet which can be accessed only by a password is most to be trusted. Obviously, sites recommended by the course supervisor can also be trusted. Indeed, some universities are themselves providing guidance on evaluating websites as part of a specific course on Internet access.

Assessing one's authorities must remain one of the most difficult aspects of the research problem. All that one can do in the way of ferreting out information – from one's instructor, or the dust-jacket, or the reviews – is subject to the arbitrament of judgement. And the trouble with judgement, as A. E. Housman observed, is that if one has not got it, one never misses it. If Professor X is after all no good, some people will never find that out. But at least safety can be sought in numbers, and in a certain scepticism. Reliance on these allies will save a student from falling too easy a prey to Calvin Hoffman's view of Shakespeare, or a Marxist's view of Western society.

* Tunku Varadarajan, 'Surf for Both Sides of the Coin', *Interface*, 30 December 1998.

Chapter 4

Taking notes

The labour of taking notes requires the utmost exactitude and discipline. Without a strict organization, the process can degenerate very easily into chaos. Supposing one approaches the matter carelessly – or naturally. One might simply jot down ideas, facts, opinions as they come, into a notebook, without reference to where they were obtained, or whether they are one's own ideas or those extracted from the writer. One would then be left, several books later, with a mass of unsortable, unverifiable material, some of which could not even be assigned to its original source. The physical difficulties of reshaping material which has been entered consecutively into a notebook are obvious enough; and the labour of rechecking a badly taken note (what I mean by this term will be apparent later in the chapter) is almost too painful to contemplate. So the job has to be done well, first time; and for that, two points must be established: the necessity for note-cards, and for a systematized mode of noting down information.

Note-cards

First, the note-cards. They are the answer to the notebook problem. The best practice is to use 6 × 4 in. cards. This is because it is convenient to use (of the standard sizes) a different one from the 5 × 3 in. bibliography cards, to avoid confusion, and because there is more room for note-taking on the larger cards. (A very large handwriting might require an 8 × 5 in. size, but normally 6 × 4 in. is ample.) A single note is taken on each card; a note consisting of one idea.

What are the benefits of this system? They are twofold. Note-cards can be rejected; and they can be rearranged. These are immense advantages; for we can say with certainty of all research, that too many notes will be taken, and in the wrong order. Researchers begin by taking notes of everything that they think might be useful. Some of the material will prove to be superseded by later material; some will prove to be, quite simply, not as useful or relevant as was first thought likely; some will have to be pruned, or excised in the interests of space. *Waste is inseparable from research*. But it is simplicity itself to reject unwanted notes from the sheaf that has been accumulated. Rearrangement is facilitated even more. There is no way of ensuring that one takes notes in the identical order to that in which they will appear in the finished work. Therefore, one has to shuffle the pack. This is very easy, if one has a pack, and not the refractory pages of a notebook, each page containing several notes of varying usefulness.

I labour the point, but it is worth labouring. And I add that all this applies with astronomically mounting force to longer projects. One might just manage to control one's material, old-style, if one is writing up a term paper on the basis of a single authoritative book. But for a long-term, ambitious piece of research, covering a variety of sources, the concept is ridiculous. Not to use note-cards is evidence of a horse-and-buggy mentality.

The system of note-taking

What should go on to the note-cards? One idea only, certainly, else the advantages of atomization are lost. But the techniques of recording the idea must be rigorously applied. Essentially, each card contains three items of information: a descriptive label, or some identifying phrase; the main body of the note itself; and the reference to the source. A sample card is shown in Figure 4. That is the simplest form which a note-card could take. There is a heading, relating the card to the theme the writer is pursuing; the note itself, a direct quotation; and the reference to its source. It should be noted that the source is identified as simply as possible. There is no need to copy out in full: M. C. Bradbrook, *Themes and Conventions of Elizabethan Tragedy*, p. 54. The student has already made a full note of all publication details in the Bibliography. But if any *other* work by M. C. Bradbrook is being used, the title will have to be identified, at least briefly. The note might then be written: Bradbrook, *Themes*, p. 54. The page number is a precise but necessary narrowing down of the reference. It has to be possible for the researcher to check on the notes, *and for a future reader to check on the researcher.* The whole foundation of scholarship rests on full and accurate identification of the means whereby one has arrived at one's conclusions. Hence the need to record the details which will later be recorded in one's footnotes.

Precision is called for in writing out the main body of the note, a matter we have now to consider in greater detail. There are in fact three types of notes that one can take: a direct quotation, as in the example; a paraphrase or summary of the original passage; and the writer's own opinions. These must be rigidly distinguished.

Let us now consider the circumstances in which one chooses a direct quotation or a paraphrase. Why does one take the note originally? Because, obviously, one considers the point of sufficient importance. But it may be important for different reasons. The original writer may have made a classic, and succinct, statement of the position; it is so well expressed that the language cannot be improved on. Here a direct quotation is in order. Or the statement, even if badly expressed, may be so fundamental to the writer's position that it should be quoted in its entirety. Again, statements in which every word counts – as in a legal or philosophic context – should be noted exactly.

There are, however, many more instances in which it is quite unnecessary to retain the exact words of the original writer. Very often a whole chapter can be rendered down to a few succinct sentences. Large quantities of data can be summarized in a few

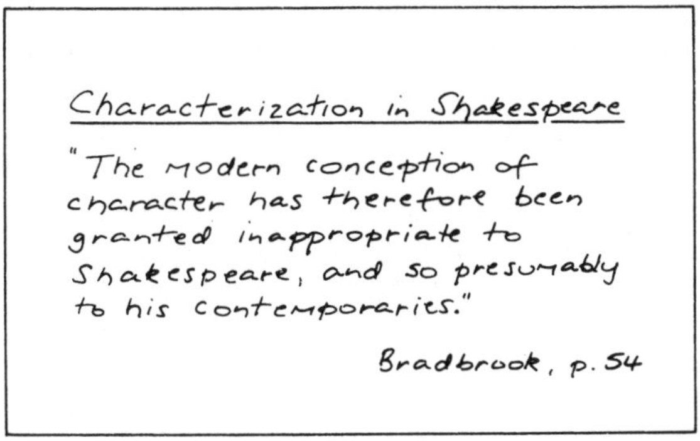

Figure 4. Simple specimen note-card.

generalizations. One paraphrases a passage for the importance of its *content*; one quotes it directly for the additional importance of its *mode of expression*.

In either case, the form is precise. An original quotation should be followed in all respects. If the text uses American or outmoded spelling, it should be copied scrupulously. An error or fatuity in the text should be copied, and followed with [*sic*] which means 'thus in the original'. If anything has been omitted from the passage copied, the fact should be indicated with ellipsis marks: three spaced full stops, preceded by a space, are used for ellipsis within a sentence, thus (. . .). If a considerable amount is omitted, a line or more of verse, or a paragraph or more of prose, this fact should be indicated by a single line of spaced full stops. If words have to be inserted to make sense of a passage, they should be enclosed in square brackets [ ] to distinguish them from the parentheses ( ) that might occur naturally in the text quoted. Square brackets are an indication always of an editorial intervention of some kind: that is, an interpolation by the writer of explanatory matter, or comment, into the text being dealt with. The complete quotation, with or without excisions or additions, should be enclosed in single quotation marks, and any quotations within it should be enclosed in double quotation marks, the writer making this change if necessary.

A paraphrase takes a precise form in that it is written down without quotation marks. This is not a verbal quibble. The researcher has to feel absolute confidence in the notes. If the quotation marks are present, that is proof that the quotation is an exact copy of the original; if quotation marks are not present, that is proof that the words are the researcher's own. It should be strongly emphasized here that the words must be genuinely the researcher's own, and show that the thought has been assimilated and not merely slightly reworded. A good plan is to read the passage through carefully, think about it a moment or two, then lay it aside and write the note without looking at the actual text, then check again to make sure that the original author has not been misrepresented. The positive and negative implications of the presence or absence of quotation marks are, then, far-reaching. But, it may be objected, surely students can tell their own words from someone else's anyway? No, they cannot. Notes taken a few weeks or months previously may have been, to all intents and purposes, written by an entirely different person. It is simply not possible to read one's own writing, after the lapse of some time, and distinguish with complete confidence in all cases between one's own words and another's. Without the apparatus I have outlined above, without the reliance on exact techniques, students will always face a twinge of doubt when they confront their notes, and come to write them up in their pages. They are then faced with unpleasing alternatives. Suppose their memory is at fault, they may advance their own paraphrase as an exact quotation – and thus blur or mar a statement where every word counts. Or they may do the reverse, and borrow another writer's exact words without acknowledgement, which in the scholarly context is just plain dishonest. Or they may avoid these pitfalls and look up the passage again – which is pure waste of time; they might just as well have got it right in the first place.

It should be emphasized at this point that in taking their notes students must guard themselves very carefully against the charge of plagiarism. The necessity of being certain whether one's own words or the author's are being used, and of avoiding paraphrase which is so close to the original as to amount to plagiarism, has already been mentioned. Even in summary, however, where the words are indubitably one's own, one must be careful to note the exact source of the information, since due acknowledgement will have to be made, in the paper, of ideas, theories or obscure facts. Failure to make this acknowledgement is just as much plagiarism as the borrowing of another author's exact words. One should therefore be extremely careful to note the page references. It is perhaps as well to mention here that it is a great convenience to mark on the note-card, where the break occurs, if a quotation extends across two pages. This may be done by inserting two parallel lines, thus //, where the page change occurs, or by inserting the number of the new page in parentheses, as in the following example: 'Ideas of tolerance came // to the West only after two or three centuries of literacy and visual Gutenberg culture.' Or 'Ideas of tolerance came (p. 303) to the West . . .'. This practice will be found useful if the writer later decides to use only part of the quotation.

So much for the vital distinction between direct quotation and paraphrase, and for the dangers of plagiarism. The third type of note, personal comment by the researcher, is an extremely valuable record of stray ideas that flash across the mind in the process of note-taking, and which can easily be lost if not quickly noted down; but they have to be labelled to avoid confusion. The same point applies as before. The intrusion of one's own ideas among those of Professor X may lead, months later, to the confident claim that the professor's ideas are one's own, or vice versa. Since one tends to assimilate ideas, the delusion is easy. I recommend, therefore, that all personal comment should be preceded by one's initials. Such a note-card looks amusingly like a fragment of Boswellian dialogue – but the techniques have dispelled any possibility of confusion.

One last point. It is convenient, and often useful, to number one's cards consecutively. This makes possible cross-reference in one's notes: as with an annotation, 'See 51 and 73'.

A more sophisticated version of a note, then, might look something like what is shown in Figure 5. The note-taker has entered in its original form a well-expressed statement. At the same time certain doubts as to the continuing truth of the observation have been jotted down, and a few pointers for future reference have been added. Later on the suggestion has been followed up (cards 120–6) and it has been found possible to add a cross-reference at the foot of the original card, No. 89.

Photocopying or printing out material

Increasingly, students are discovering the convenience of photocopying at least some of the information used in preparation for writing their research papers. They may use a printout facility

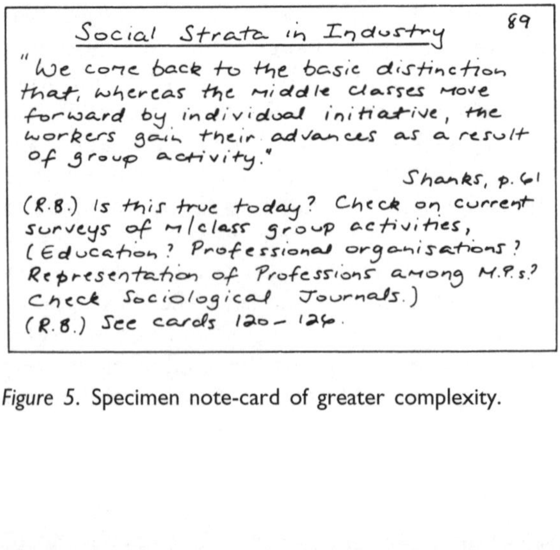

Social Strata in Industry 89

"We come back to the basic distinction that, whereas the middle classes move forward by individual initiative, the workers gain their advances as a result of group activity."

Shanks, p. 61

(R.B.) Is this true today? Check on current surveys of m/class group activities, (Education? Professional organisations? Representation of Professions among M.P.s? Check Sociological Journals.)

(R.B.) See cards 120–126.

Figure 5. Specimen note-card of greater complexity.

with CD-ROMs or the Internet to copy blocks of text or illustrations. Photocopies or printouts are particularly useful for such
material as charts, tables of statistics, maps or illustrations. These
can be valuable for retention for closer study of portions of the
material particularly important to the student's theme. These
sections may need to be looked at carefully later in the research,
when more knowledge has been accumulated and the student's
viewpoint may have shifted.

There are, however, certain dangers (apart from the expense
involved!). Too much photocopying or printing may consist of
the mindless accumulation of piles of unassimilated pages. Without
careful documentation, later attribution of sources may be difficult. Finally, the student may once again encounter the problem
stated at the beginning of this chapter of the physical difficulties
of shaping the material.

I will take these points one at a time. First, it is good practice
to ask oneself before photocopying or printing: can I summarize
the main ideas on note-cards, which will be more handy for future
reference? The same question can be applied to the number of
pages reproduced, so as to reduce the material as much as possible.
A rigorous application of these principles will ensure that the
material is not unassimilated, since its relevance to the theme will
be constantly checked. After it has been reproduced it may, of
course, be gone through and underlined or highlighted to bring
out the important points. Indeed, in this respect the reproduction
is superior to the original. The writer may use it, in effect, as a
notebook, and scribble comments in the margin with no fear of
mistaking these words or ideas for those of the writer. This is a
treatment that obviously cannot be applied to a library book, and
that one would be loath to apply to a book of one's own, except
possibly a very cheap and expendable paperback.

Second, the student should get into the habit of writing full
details of the book, article, CD-ROM or website from which the
material came, on the first page, and of stapling the pages together
at once, so that they do not become mixed up with other material. Thus attribution can be properly made in the research paper
and the dangers of plagiarism avoided.

Last, it may be found that the use of a few note-cards, referring to the reproduced material, will help to overcome the physical
problems of the need to shuffle the notes. For example, a note-
card for each of the main ideas, with a reference 'see printout

p. 000 for further details', will enable the material to be inserted into the correct place in the argument of the research paper.

By using these methods the student can gain all the advantages of photocopying without losing the advantages of note-cards.

And so the pile of cards accumulates. The more cards in the pile, the more manifestly efficient the whole procedure is; for the sheer bulk of the operation fractures a less orderly structure. The efficiency of the procedure rests on two principles: the atomization of knowledge, and the absolute reliance the researcher can place on the techniques of coding knowledge.

Chapter 5

Composing the paper

The mass of data has now to be converted to a draft. We can usefully think of this operation as having three phases: making a skeleton outline, preparing an initial rough draft and improving the rough draft.

Making a skeleton outline

This is the most intellectually exacting part of the whole process. Order must be imposed upon chaos, and it is at this precise point that the forces of chaos and order meet. Some two or three hours of uninterrupted thought should be set aside to consider the matter; it is not to be tackled in a stray half-hour; once the material has been set into a form, the mould will be hard to break and harder to alter. The writer has the task of reading, very rapidly, and very lightly, over the notes. Not much of the detail, of course, can be remembered at this stage. The aim is to impregnate the mind with as much as possible of the data. Only then can the material begin to be shaped.

Shape implies arrangement and rejection. The latter is hard. It is understandable that students should want to use a great deal of their notes. People feel a natural and human desire to demonstrate the full extent of their labours. But, as I have said before, waste is inseparable from research. Students must reconcile themselves to this, and be prepared ruthlessly to abandon large tracts of notes should they prove to be superfluous or unacceptable.

Such a decision can only be taken in the light of a constant brooding on the *purpose* of the project. Even now, at this late stage, the exact title may not be fixed. If it is, this title should be allowed to dominate the choice of material; if not, the mental energies of the writer should be directed towards crystallizing the title. At this stage, the problem is normally one of restriction. The writer has a full conspectus of the notes. The question must be asked: 'Can I carry out the project on the lines which I first intended? Or, with this mass of material, should I limit my scope?' Perhaps a historical résumé has to be compressed, so as to allow the major period to be properly studied. Perhaps some interesting and worthwhile side issues have to be abandoned. Perhaps a complex and controversial problem looks to be getting out of control; so the writer decides to play safe and concentrate only on those aspects of the matter that can be adequately handled. All these problems are intimately connected in a chain that extends from title to outline, from outline to selection of material.

I assume these problems to be provisionally settled, and turn to the details of the outline problem. This problem I define as *the search for internal form*. Every topic has a natural form, and it is the business of the writer to explore and clarify this form. I can best illustrate the point with some examples.

(a)   The easiest of forms occurs within historic topics. The secret of history, as Churchill says, is chronology. So one has simply to begin at the beginning (whenever this point is judged to be) and carry on. There may be a secondary problem of judgement in dividing time into phases, but this is no great matter. Thus a general analysis of a historic phenomenon would break the subject down into Origins; Development; Results. The Munich Crisis can very reasonably be judged to start (as far as any historic problem can be so judged) from 1919, the date of the Treaty of Versailles. The period 1919–38 covers the origins of the Crisis, and can reasonably be subdivided into two phases: 1919–33 (the accession to power of Hitler) and 1933–8. As for the results, one would certainly have to consider its effect on the beginning of the War, in 1939, and perhaps take the question as far as 1940–1. After that the question becomes too speculative. So a likely outline for a paper on the 1938 Munich Crisis looks like this:

Part I: Origins (A) 1919–33, (B) 1933–8
Part II: The Crisis
Part III: The Aftermath 1938–40

We can add to this a brief Introduction, which states the main purpose and direction of the paper; and a Conclusion which returns to the purpose statement in the Introduction and reviews it in the light of the material examined.

All this is pleasant and convenient, and a great incitement to work in the field of history. It is equally true that a chronological approach works well with a variety of topics. Thus a paper on 'Poets of the 1914–18 War' might well deal with the host of names by grouping them around Brooke and Owen, representing the spirit (if one likes) of 1914 and 1917. This would be a fair start to the outline problem. Later one could face the question: does the quality and significance of the poetry of 1915–16 demand a section devoted to the transition?

(b) But chronology, unfortunately, is not the whole of history. The problem for historians – and I take it as a model for anyone classifying material – is also the ordering of events that occur simultaneously. To make their statements even approximately coherent, they must divide the activities of people into compartments labelled 'political', 'social', 'art', 'economics', etc. They must explain, as best they can, the interactions of these compartments. This analysis of life is artificial, like all analytical processes; and its justification is that the human mind can only communicate by imposing an artificial order on an incredibly complex mass of data. 'History', says Burckhardt, 'is the record of what one age finds notable in another.' Such is history; but the same act of judgement is necessary to select and order material in other fields.

Thus, the purely chronological outline I have mentioned in my first example is only apparently adequate. It is certainly a promising start. I doubt if a significantly better one could be devised. But it still leaves one with the problem of subdividing within the chronological framework. There the writer must search for an acceptable internal form.

In the specimen paper on Nazi Propaganda, reproduced below, the writer drew up a scheme combining chronology and analysis:

1 General definition of propaganda.
   Its relationship to the twentieth century.
2 Division of the role of Nazi Propaganda into three stages:
   (i) its role when they were a minority party;

(ii) its role when they controlled the organs of government;

(iii) war propaganda.

The decision was then taken to exclude the third category. This illustrates the ever-present need, mentioned at the beginning of this chapter, to exclude material, hitherto seen as promising and relevant.

3   Chronological treatment:

(i)   propaganda before 1933;

(ii) propaganda after 1933.

Within this framework the propaganda methods are to be examined separately for each section.

4   Questions raised by Nazi Propaganda.

In this example the starting point is chronology but within that framework a further analysis has been found necessary.

(c) The title itself often affords some clue to the necessary internal form. Indeed, some writers will be well content with simply defining the paper's title. Take, for example, a title containing the term 'Primitive Art'. The term has to be defined before it can be applied; and the writer might well settle in the end for the title 'Some Characteristics of Primitive Art'. The subject might be analysed thus:

1   Primitive art exists from earliest times.
      (*But* it is found in tribal societies today.)
2   It may be crude, rough, unsophisticated.
      (*But* some primitive art is highly sophisticated.)
3   It is intimately connected with religious rites.
      (*But* how is this distinguished from later religious art?)
4   It is functionally connected with religion, having no base in self-expression.
      (*But* does the controlling purpose of primitive art negate the idea of self-expression?)
5   It represents nowadays a sophisticated and deliberate return to older methods of expression.
      (*But* is not this pseudo-Primitivism?)

Here the writer has laid out the ideas in accordance with a movement of sorts. The analysis moves from the obvious to the less
obvious, early to modern. By the nature of the subject, not only
the arguments but also the counter-arguments have to be considered. There is here a rough analytical framework that can serve
either as a complete paper in itself, or as a starting point to a
larger project. It is naturally possible to focus at length on any
one point – say 4 – that seems the crux of the matter; reducing
the other points to lesser issues that can be disposed of in the
Introduction.

Generally, any difficulty inherent in the title should be faced *at
once*. And in the above example the objections to each element
in the analysis have been dealt with as they occur.

(d)   One final example will serve to underline the need to analyse
an issue into parts, and thus pave the way for a later synthesis.
The student had taken the topic: 'The Flow of Traffic in Large
Towns'. Clearly the title indicated a complex of unruly problems.
The first step was to impose the simplest ordering of data, that
is, 'Problems' and 'Solutions'. The next was to subdivide the problems, followed by the solutions. An outline of the paper looked
like this:

I   *Introduction*. General statement of the problem.

II   *Aspects of the problem*.

  (a) Simultaneous use of local and through traffic.
  (b) Speed limits and traffic lights which slow down the flow.
  (c) Intersections.
  (d) Parked cars.
  (e) Loading and servicing of shopping areas.
  (f) Pedestrians, especially at crossings.

III *Attempted solutions*.

  (a) The Slough Experiment.
  (b) Various other solutions tried in Britain and abroad, as:
      (1) Urban motorways over, under or round the town to
           take traffic.
      (2) Roads from suburbs with tidal flow (three lanes in,
           one lane out, in the morning: and the converse in the
           evening).

(3) Clover under- or over-passes for intersections or, where too expensive, computer-controlled traffic signals.

(4) Multi-storey or underground off-street parking.

IV   *Conclusion.* General trends and prospects in the planners' fight to keep traffic moving.

The material here was refractory but a logical movement had again been observed. In the Problems, it was from roads and vehicles to people's use of them. In the Solutions, the breakdown was first broadly historical to take in the Slough Experiment, and then corresponded as far as possible to the analysis of the Problems.

These examples cannot be reduced to a series of precepts. Every topic is a unique problem; it demands to be appraised in its own terms. What the student has to do is to develop the capacity to feel for the natural form inherent in every topic.

The student who is really anxious to develop this faculty, and there is none more important for really excellent work, will find it useful to study examples where it is displayed by others. Leading articles in the best journals and newspapers offer useful case material. One can also get into the habit of analysing the way material has been shaped for TV programmes. *Walden* on ITV was a useful example of a format which frequently moved from general exposition of a problem, in an introductory section, to the advancement of argument and counter-argument in a discussion or interview. A keen observation of the various methods used by experienced practitioners, to impose order and form on refractory material, will enable the student to develop his or her own skills.

The examples I have suggested here as case material are generally of limited length. More ambitious examples to follow can be found in the best reports of Select Committees, where a great bulk of material, collected over a fairly long period, and representing, of necessity, very opposing points of view, has to be rendered into clear, readable form, leading to clear recommendations.

A model of its kind, and worthy of study purely for its form, is the *Warnock Report on Human Fertilisation and Embryology.**

---

* Department of Health and Social Security, *Report of the Committee of Inquiry into Human Fertilisation and Embryology* (Chairman Dame Mary Warnock, DBE), presented to Parliament July 1984 (London: HMSO, 1984).

Here the writer, Dame Mary Warnock, was faced with a mass of difficult material involving technical definitions but also complex moral and legal issues. An exceedingly clear form was imposed on the report.

Chapter 1 set out the background to the inquiry and its terms of reference, defined words used in the terms of reference, and divided the task into two parts. These were to consider (a) processes designed to benefit the individual and (b) the pursuit of knowledge designed to benefit society at large.

Thus a clear twofold division was imposed at the start and this was followed, with Chapters 2–8 concerned mainly with the first of these tasks and Chapters 9–12 with the second.

Chapter 2 considered the state of infertility, whether it was a condition meriting treatment, and the scope of services for its alleviation. It drew the clear conclusion that it should be treated.

Chapters 3–8 considered, one by one, the possible techniques for doing this, the medical and legal questions involved with them, and the ethical arguments against. In the case of each technique, clear definitions were given and a clear conclusion was drawn.

Chapters 9–12 shifted to the question of benefits to society at large, and considered the wider use of these techniques, both now and in the future. The scientific and moral implications raised by the use of human embryos for research were also addressed.

Chapter 13 gave clear recommendations for future policy.

Throughout, the report concentrated on principles rather than details, and made a clear distinction between areas where legislation would be needed, and those where only guidance or a general change of attitudes would be necessary. On the most difficult question of all, the moral dimension, the consistent approach throughout was that strongly, but not universally, held moral views are not binding on the formulation of public policy, since an individual holding them can refuse to participate in the particular practice under consideration.

A list of recommendations followed, with paragraph references to the relevant sections of the main text, thus binding the report together into a clear and consistent whole.

I have given a full analysis of this particular report because the material presents difficulties greater than any students can be expected to find in their own work. In particular the writer has to deal with a number of very technical issues, yet render them comprehensible to a lay readership. She has also to address herself to moral issues and give full weight to very strongly held views which oppose the recommendations she finally advances. The consistency, clarity and logic of the argument throughout make it a model for students, and the fact that it is intended for a lay readership makes it useful as a model, even for those whose own studies may lie in a very different field.

Students may also, of course, find that there are government reports or similar official documents related to their own fields, in which they will find useful models for their own writing. It is the general principle that is important: to be alert to examples of good structure and to spend a few minutes analysing what it is that has made them good.

Writing the rough draft

With the outline prepared, the student should assemble the notes in readiness for the rough draft. They should be sorted out into the order corresponding to the outline's demands, and the unwanted cards set aside. This decision should definitely precede the actual business of writing. There should be, at this stage, a clear-cut task of writing up a series of notes, in a predetermined order, into consecutive prose. It is worthwhile repeating here that the cards can easily be arranged into this order so that the writing becomes relatively simple.

Little need be said about this writing stage. As mentioned in the Introduction, I have no intention of telling my readers about basic composition. One point should, however, be made and that is the need to avoid giving offence by the use of 'he' and the variety of forms connected with it, when the reference could as well apply to a woman as a man. Since English is deficient in not possessing any form of neutral pronoun, other than 'one' which can become clumsy if repeated too often, considerable ingenuity needs to be exercised to overcome the problem. It will be found that in many cases the use of an impersonal phrase or the passive voice will help: thus, instead of 'he must take care' one can use 'care must be taken' or 'it is necessary to'. The impersonal 'the' can usually be substituted for 'his'. Often the plural can be used: 'students', instead of 'the student', and with it the non-sexist 'their'. What must be avoided is ambiguity or a hideous distortion of grammar by such usages as 'their' with a singular noun.

Two practical suggestions on the writing stage ought to be considered. The student will be well advised to use wide-lined paper, or to write on alternate lines, to leave plenty of space for alterations or additions. Secondly, only one paragraph might be written on each sheet of paper, leaving space at the end for finishing incomplete paragraphs, or inserting additional material, afterthoughts, clarifying sentences, and so on. Certain long quotations may be referred to briefly and filled in later. Moreover, the whole paragraph may in the final version be assigned to a different part of the paper. Students who do not adopt this method should at least leave some spaces between each paragraph – and leave a considerable *margin*. One of the needless frustrations of revising a draft is to find no space available for afterthoughts.

In effect, by adopting the practices recommended above, the student is gaining some of the advantages offered by word processing. As technology is advancing so rapidly, most students will in fact have access to a word processor. If so, they should certainly use it.

A word processor is the finest technical help to reshaping and reorganizing one's thoughts. One can type a rough draft rapidly, knowing that one can, with the utmost ease, make corrections, deletions and additions. One can also move whole paragraphs or sections around to improve the flow of the argument. There is no greater incentive to the improvement of formal structure and argument than the speed and ease with which this can be done.

I do not intend here to give any exposition of word processing techniques, since these will vary with the particular equipment and programs to which the student has access. I shall content myself with urging students to gain the benefit of this technology if they can. One caution is worth advancing, and that is to be sure to 'save' the text at frequent intervals, and to keep a back-up copy. There are few things as irritating as to have spent a couple of hours typing a text and then lose it, through a power cut before it is 'saved', or later, through loss of, or damage to, the disk.

Improving the rough draft

Turning the rough draft into the final draft is a business which needs a cold critical eye. I recommend that if possible the student should leave the rough draft for a while – Kipling left his for a year at a time – to grow 'cold'. A few days is better than nothing. It is vital to approach the rough draft as though it were someone else's. It might very well be read to a friend – Swift read his drafts to his servants, and Molière to his cook. The point of this is that it is psychologically very difficult to criticize one's own work. One's blind spots in composition tend to recur; and the tendency to approve one's own work is strong. But if the draft is 'cold' it is easier to approach it impartially; and an outside opinion is better still. In revising the rough draft, one ought to concentrate on two aspects: the verifying of footnotes, quotations and illustrations, and those aspects of the paper in which precision is essential; and the flow, and grammatical accuracy, of the writing.

Getting ready one's footnotes, illustrations, etc., and checking their accuracy, needs no explanation. Nonetheless, the importance of this labour is central. 'Accuracy', said Whitehead, 'is the morality of the scientist.' It is part of the morality of the researcher.

The quality of 'flow' stems naturally from a well-organized outline. But this in itself is not sufficient. The transition from paragraph to paragraph is an important technique. Usually, not invariably, the opening sentence of a paragraph – the 'topic sentence' – announces the theme of the paragraph to follow. Often it is possible to make the topic sentence link up with the last sentence of the preceding paragraph. Within the paragraph itself, a succession of guide words (such as 'however', 'consequently', 'on the other hand', 'moreover', 'thus', 'finally') help conduct the reader across the territory to be traversed. A well-written paper, in my view, is not so much one that is grammatically impeccable – that should be taken for granted – as one in which the chain of evidence and reasoning is easy to follow. No unreasonable demands should be made upon the reader. A common fault, for example, is for the researcher to become so immersed in the topic as to refer in the paper to personages, events and terms that are obscure in the extreme. Unless one can assume a degree of expert knowledge in the reader, this is a provoking irritant. And it is courteous to remind even the enlightened reader. It is also a common fault of inexperienced writers to suppose that because they themselves know what they mean, their reader must automatically do so as well. Hence the value of reading the rough draft to a friend – and if that friend knows nothing of the topic, so much the better. The devastating interruption 'Who's he?' or 'What's that?' can remind the writer forcefully of the perennial duty to readers to make their lives as easy and pleasant as possible.

Chapter 6

The final version

Advice is given here in accordance with generally recognized practice, and especially with the recommendations of the *MLA Handbook for Writers of Research Papers*, Fifth edition, Joseph Gibaldi (New York, 1999). It should be emphasized, however, that some institutions favour particular conventions. Publishers, for example, often have their own in-house style. Students must ensure that any particular regulations of their own institutions are followed. The advice given here is in default of such regulations being supplied.

One preliminary caution should be offered before any start is made on typing the final manuscript. Literary history abounds in cases of lost manuscripts. It can happen to anyone. The practice of taking a photocopy, or printing out a second copy, or having a back-up disk virtually eliminates the difficulties arising from such loss, and should always be followed. In any event, a copy has uses outside its insurance value; it enables the task of making the final check to be shared, and permits a clean version of the text to be retained, free from marginalia.

Format

In its final form the research paper should be presented as a typescript. Conventionally the paper used is standard A4 (297 mm × 210 mm). The typing of the text should be double-spaced and as uniform as possible, in terms of line length and number of lines per page. Advice here is given for a typed manuscript. Most students will be using a word processor and can adapt the instructions for format to suit the particular packages used by their machines. Whichever method is used, care must be taken to decide on a format which provides ample margins and ample top and bottom spaces. Allow 2 to 3 cm in each case, with the left-hand margin 4 cm wide, to allow for binding. The first page should have a margin of 5 cm at the top, and the title centred and typed in capitals. Pages should be numbered consecutively, either in the top right-hand corner, or in the centre at the top. It is a good plan to type one's own name before the number of each page, to guard against any of the pages being mislaid, or confused with those of another paper. The beginning of each new paragraph should be indented four spaces and the space between paragraphs should be the normal double-spacing, unless a decided break in subject matter is to be indicated.

Certain conventions of presentation should be observed throughout. Quotation marks are used to draw attention to a word or phrase which is under discussion, as: 'it is permissible to write "and others" after the name of the first author', where the words 'and others' are being singled out for consideration. If these words are used within a quotation, double quotation marks are used, otherwise single, as above. Where italics would be used for emphasis, if the full resources of the printer were available, a single underline should be employed. It should be noted, however, that too great a use of italics is out of keeping with a scholarly piece of work. A single underline should also be used for the titles of published works, and for foreign words used in the text, unless these are so much used as to have become anglicized. Usage for dates should be consistent. Practice varies, but the format 14 February 1970 is gaining ground. The same consistency is required for numerals, where it is customary for those of fewer than three digits, and those beginning a sentence, to be spelled out.

Care must also be taken in the transcription of quotations. If the advice given above has been followed, the quotation will already be in the correct form on the note-card. It remains to insert it correctly into the text of the research paper. One must first distinguish between short quotations, fewer than sixty words of prose, and no more than two lines of verse, and longer quotations.

Short prose quotations may be run into the text without any introductory punctuation. They should be enclosed in single quotation marks. A quotation within a short quotation should be enclosed in double quotation marks. The question of the punctuation at the end of a quotation, in quotation marks, sometimes gives trouble. The rule is a simple one: if the punctuation is a necessary part of the original quotation, as in the case of a question mark or exclamation mark, it should be retained before the quotation marks. Otherwise the punctuation is that of the original sentence, in which the quotation is included, and comes after the quotation marks. This may, in fact, lead to double punctuation. Examples will make this clearer.

Examples

Who can deny the effectiveness of the description of Cleopatra as 'a lass unparalleled'?

(The quotation is not a question, therefore the question mark comes after the quotation mark, as part of the original sentence.)

We all remember Caesar's famous question 'Et tu, Brute?'.

(The quotation is a question, therefore the question mark comes before the quotation mark, and the original sentence is completed with its own full stop.) If we turn this into a question, as below, we shall see the double punctuation more clearly:

Which of us does not remember Caesar's famous question 'Et tu, Brute?'?

Short verse quotations are similarly run into the text. If the quotation extends over two lines, it is the practice to indicate the break, not by setting out, but by a slash followed by a capital letter, as in the following example:

An example of this imagery is 'The hearts/That spaniel'd me at heels'.

Longer quotations must not be incorporated into a sentence in such a way as to break its continuity, since the reader cannot be expected to wait for the end of the sentence until after the quotation. They may, however, be introduced by a colon, indicating that they form an explanation, or extension, of the preceding sentence. They must begin on a new line. They are not enclosed in quotation marks. Some way must, therefore, be found of differentiating them from the main text. Practice on this varies, but the most frequently used method is to have a deeper indentation, often on both sides, and to use single spacing. Any quotation within the long quotation will be set off from it by single quotation marks, and, if there is a further quotation within that, by double quotation marks, following the rules given above for short quotations.

Long verse quotations present fewer problems, since they are already marked off by their form from a prose text. They also are typed without quotation marks, more fully indented, following their own verse or line format, and single spaced.

If it is desired to give a reference to the text, within the main body of the paper (line reference for verse or page reference), this is given in brackets, after the punctuation of the quotation, and with no punctuation of its own.

It is sometimes necessary to indicate, in the middle of a quotation, that material has been omitted. This is shown in prose quotations by three spaced full stops. In the case of verse quotations the three spaced full stops are typed at the end of the line before the omission.

The preliminary pages of front matter

The first page is the title page. This simply gives the details of title and author, and if required the name of the course and instructor. Next comes the outline. This is an abstract of the contents, prepared in complete sentence form. It should be an accurate summary of the main points established, while indicating the structure of the paper. Finally, it may be desirable to add a table of contents. Obviously, certain papers are fairly simple and written in continuous form. No table is here necessary. But if the paper is a more ambitious affair, containing chapters, illustrations or appendixes, then a table of contents is in order.

Additional material

The question of additional material (such as photographs, diagrams, graphs, statistical tables) must be briefly raised here. The presentation of such material, especially photographs, is a purely technical matter which must be left to the judgement of the writer. It is outside my brief to offer specific advice on this.

I do, however, stress that the business of setting up illustrations should be taken very seriously. Illustrative material should be carefully chosen and prepared so as to give information. If, for example, a diagram relates specifically to a point explained in the text, it is sound policy to submit the text and diagram to a friend and ask: does the diagram, in fact, enlighten? Does it adequately complement the text? Is it, text aside, self-explanatory on its own visual terms? And this leads us to another consideration. Obviously the basic virtues of illustration are clarity and relevance. But the student should also consider the possibilities of sheer graphic appeal. Statistical information, for example, can be presented diagrammatically with great impact. Even a hoary old device such as depicting a single figure to represent a million of the population is better than nothing. It shows that the writer is making an effort to think graphically, to present information conceived visually, not tied to verbal forms. Such a faculty is not found universally, and many people are constricted by the heavily verbal emphasis of their formal education. They could well reflect on the opportunities a research paper affords to extend their range of expression. Even a simple graph is a case in point. It is not solely a mathematical concept; it is a visual device. The possibilities of a subject can and should be explored through visual means. It should also be noted that the technical possibilities of illustrating never were greater. Through the latest techniques of reproduction, colour, typography and computer graphics, the student can intensify the projection of the theme.

A basic problem should be mentioned. Should such material be presented alongside the text, often at the cost of considerable disarray? Or should it be relegated to the end of the paper, and presented in the form of an appendix or series of appendixes? Clearly the latter is more convenient for the writer; the former may be more convenient for the reader. The writer should ask the question: does the material throw any direct light upon the point considered in the text? Is it desirable for the reader to view with ease text and illustrations together? If so, then the writer should make an effort to accommodate the reader. But if the essential function of the illustrative material is to reinforce rather than to enlighten – this applies especially to statistical tables – then the writer should banish them to an appendix, and refuse to allow them to clutter up the text.

Documentation: footnotes

The major problem in the final presentation of the text is the matter of documentation. The central issue is quite clear. The value of a research paper consists very largely in the sources used. Therefore, these sources must be acknowledged in two ways. The Bibliography listed at the end is a general acknowledgement; the footnotes spaced throughout the paper specifically and individually document facts and opinions referred to. Without this general and individual acknowledgement, the reader would be completely at sea. There would only be an unsubstantiated and undifferentiated mass.

What information should be documented via a footnote? The matter is quite considerably one of judgement. A fact like the date of the Battle of Waterloo requires no authority to support it. A fact like the casualty returns of the Prussians at Waterloo does. Facts in any way specialized or beyond the run of common knowledge ought to be documented. So should opinions. We ought to know the circumstances and the time when an opinion was formed. The time is particularly important as it often colours the views of the writer. (C. V. Wedgwood, for example, in the Introduction to the 1957 edition of her *The Thirty Years War* writes: 'I wrote this book in the thirties, against the background of depression at home and mounting tension abroad. The preoccupations of that unhappy time cast their shadows over its pages.') If the opinion being considered is a scholarly opinion, we must have the full details of the work cited. The authority should be cited, not left vague as 'one authority'. Clearly a direct quotation should always be footnoted. (Except the non-specialist allusion. One does not give chapter and verse for a quotation from *Hamlet*, unless one is writing on *Hamlet*.) A paraphrase of a quotation must also be footnoted. Finally, the sources of technical information such as tables, diagrams and charts should also be acknowledged.

Conventions somewhat differ on the form the footnotes take. It is agreed that a single numeral, typed a single roller space above the line (and invariably at the *end* of the quotation or material to be documented, after punctuation, if any), should draw the reader's attention to the existence of the footnote. This numeral is then repeated at the foot of the page, or the end of the paper, and followed by a statement of the authority. But the numbering series can take various forms. It is permissible to number foot-notes on a page-by-page basis: that is, given three footnotes on a page, one numbers 1, 2 and 3, then begins again with 1 on the next page. Or one can number them consecutively to the end of the section. Or one can number them consecutively throughout the whole paper, a method sometimes applied to entire books.

Practice varies also on the location of the footnotes. The term 'footnotes' is a sufficient indication of the normal placing of the notes. Still, there is a growing tendency for notes to be assembled either at the end of a chapter, or at the end of the entire work. Opinions differ on the usefulness of this tendency. It is certainly inconvenient to have to turn to another page for an authority. Yet a thicket of footnotes at the bottom of the page has little aesthetic appeal to the reader, especially when they afford only a mechanical liturgy of chapter and verse. Furthermore, it is trouble-some to type a group of footnotes; one has to allow for the space needed, and it is painfully easy to forget the need for the space altogether. Typing the notes at the end is much easier. In my opin-ion the best solution is a compromise one. Some writers divide their notes into two categories. The first category contains the routine details of documentation – author, work, page number. The second embraces notes that are essentially explanatory – comment, additional quotation, illustrative material that cannot readily be absorbed into the main text. Category two should plainly be at the foot of the page; category one can safely be rele-gated to the end. This seems to me a sensible and civilized discrimination, and I recommend it to my readers. It does, how-ever, assume a distinctive symbolism for each category of foot-note. The writer adopting this division must be prepared to use an asterisk (or some other symbol) as opposed to numerals, to distinguish one category from the other.

If the writer prefers to adopt the method of typing footnotes at the foot of the page, certain points should be borne in mind. First, one may avoid the tiresome necessity of a string of foot-notes referring to the same work, when part of the function of the paper is close study of that work. One may do this after the first full footnoted reference, by brief page references in paren-theses in the main text, after the quotation marks. Thus if one is making a close study of Shakespeare's Sonnets, for example, after the first footnote giving full details of the edition used, one may give subsequent references by number and line, as: XVIII, 10–12.

This saves tiresome repetition. A second point is that it is necessary to use a consistent format in the typing. It is recommended that the footnote should be set off from the text by allowing a triple space above and by single spacing the note itself. A double space should be left between footnotes. If for any reason the note cannot be completed on the page, it should be continued on the next page, separated from the text by a single continuous line, typed one space below the last line of the text. It is obvious that a careful calculation will be needed before the start of typing a page as to how much space will be needed for footnotes, to ensure that the last line of the last footnote is above the normal margin. When the calculation has been made, a tiny pencil mark in the margin, which can later be erased, will serve as a reminder where to stop typing the main text.

Whichever system of placing the footnotes is adopted, great care must be taken in maintaining the correct format for each footnote. This is where the material collected on the bibliography cards is first used. It is important to remember that there is a distinction between a first reference to a book or article, when the full version is used, and a subsequent reference when a streamlined version is sufficient.

First reference footnotes

The information is given as on the bibliography cards, but there are differences of format.

Reference to a book

The author's name is given first, in normal order, that is initials or first name(s), followed by last name, followed by a comma. This is followed by the title of the work, in italics or underlined, and followed by a comma, unless the facts of publication, which are enclosed in parentheses, immediately follow, in which case the comma follows the parentheses. If there is an editor or translator, if an edition other than the first is used, or if the book is one of a number of volumes, this information comes after the comma and before the publication details. Publication details are enclosed in parentheses. Usage varies on what is included. It is increasingly the practice to omit the publisher's name and to give only the place and date of publication. Students should take advice on the practice favoured by their own institutions, for example by consulting a recent unpublished thesis of that institution in the library. If the publisher's name is to be included, the form is as follows: place of publication, colon, name of publisher, comma, date of publication, exactly as on the bibliography card. The first example below illustrates this. If the publisher's name is not to be included, then the place of publication alone is given, followed by a comma and the date of publication, as in the other examples below. The parentheses are followed by a comma and then the exact location of the quotation, that is the volume number, if relevant, in roman capitals, comma, page number(s), full stop.

Examples

> Humphrey Carpenter, *OUDS: A Centenary History of the Oxford University Dramatic Society 1885–1985* (Oxford: Oxford University Press, 1985), p. 178.
>
> *The Backbench Diaries of Richard Crossman*, edited by Janet Morgan (London, 1981), p. 316.
>
> E. H. Gombrich, *The Story of Art*, 12th edition, enlarged and revised (London, 1972), p. 269.
>
> C. J. Lowe and M. L. Dockrill, *The Mirage of Power*, 3 vols. (London, 1972), Vol. I, p. 18.

Reference to an article

The format used on the bibliography card should be followed exactly, except that the author's name is given in normal order and followed by a comma. Thus the second example given in Chapter 3 above will be written:

> Peter Arnott, 'Some Costume Conventions in Greek Tragedy', *Essays in Theatre*, Vol. 2, No. 1 (November 1983), pp. 3–18 (p. 15).

Reference to material from the Internet

The format used on the bibliography card should be followed exactly, except that, if there is an author, the name will be written in normal order. Thus the example given in Chapter 3 above will appear as:

Andrew L. Slayman (1999) 'A Cache of Vintage Ships', *Archaeology* [Online], Vol. 52, number 4, July/August 1999, page 2. Available from: http://www.archaeology.org/ 9907/etc/pisa. html [accessed 18 September 1999].

Second and subsequent reference footnotes

All this refers to the first appearance of an item in a footnote. Certain conventional short cuts are employed afterwards. Suppose that the first footnote is as the first example given above. The next footnote, if it refers to the same work, need not repeat the information. It is now no longer the accepted practice to use the abbreviation of the Latin forms (*ibid.* for *ibidem* 'in the same place', and *op. cit.* for *opere citato* 'in the work cited'). Instead, it is recommended practice to give the author's name and the page reference, if only one work by that author is being cited. Thus for the first example above, one would write Carpenter, p. 105. If one is referring to more than one work by the same author, it will be necessary to give a shortened form of the title. If, for example, one were using two books by Emrys Jones, say *Scenic Form in Shakespeare* and *The Origins of Shakespeare*, one might, after the first full reference footnote, use Jones, *Origins*, p. 50, and Jones, *Scenic Form*, p. 85, to distinguish them.

Where close study of a particular text is carried on throughout one or more paragraphs, it is possible to incorporate page references in brackets within the text, and thus avoid a string of repetitive footnotes. In the Specimen Paper, for example, the writer has incorporated bracketed references to *Mein Kampf* into her text.

Documentation: Bibliography

To the Bibliography belongs the place of honour at the rear of the research paper. It comes last, following the main text, the Appendixes (if any), and the Notes (if they have been assembled at the end, and not treated as footnotes). It is a formal statement of the credentials of the paper, and should be presented in the fullest and most exact form possible. Moreover, it should be honest. There are lies, damned lies and bibliographies: it is easy to draw up an imposing list of titles known more by repute than otherwise to the writer. The criterion for inclusion, however, is clear. The Bibliography (in effect the final Bibliography) should include only those sources which the researcher has actually used for the paper. It is thus different from the initial Bibliography, which was purely a stage in the preparation of the paper, and listed all possible sources. The final Bibliography lists only those sources which yielded significant material to the researcher. This does not mean that only sources actually quoted in the paper may be cited. One might, for example, read a book as important background material, yet find no opportunity of actually working part of it into one's paper, even though it has significantly enlarged one's understanding of the topic. Or one might study an obviously relevant source book, yet draw a blank as far as usable material goes; a great deal of honest research may afford only negative conclusions. In either case it is perfectly proper to cite the works one has consulted. Again, one may use only a chapter, or a part, of a work. The great thing is that the Bibliography should cite only material genuinely relevant to the topic, and genuinely consulted by the researcher.

The form of the Bibliography

Again, the details are taken from the bibliography cards. The student will now see why the information on these cards is not quite in the same format as that used for the footnotes. The bibliography card has the author's name with last name first; this makes for ease of sorting for the Bibliography, which is always presented in alphabetical order.

All items should be listed alphabetically by the last name of the author or editor. A work which has both author and editor will be listed under author, unless it is the qualities of the editing which the paper has been considering. If no author's or editor's name is available, but the work is produced by a public body, it is listed under the first important word of the name. If not even this is available, it is listed under the first important word of the title. Several titles by the same author should also be listed alphabetically from the first important word in each title. This simple classification ought to be enough for a research paper; however, sometimes a mass of detail invites a further classification. One can conveniently distinguish between books and articles. Often a Bibliography is divided into 'General' works and materials specifically related to the topic. Historians especially like to distinguish between primary and secondary sources. And the nature of the topic frequently suggests its own breakdown into areas. For the great majority of student papers, however, a simple alphabetized list will be sufficient.

The details given are exactly the same as in the footnotes, but with differences of format. Thus the author's name, or the first author's name if there is more than one, is given with the last name first, followed by a comma, followed by the first name(s) or initials, exactly as on the bibliography cards. The title is underlined, or italicized in the case of a book, or placed in single quotation marks, in the case of an article or chapter. Publishing details are given as on the bibliography card. On the question of punctuation and setting out of these details usage again varies. The important thing is to be consistent in whatever style one has chosen to adopt. Again, students are advised to check what is the preferred style of their own institutions. The two areas of difference are in the separation of the author's name from the title, and the way that the publishing details are set off from the rest. Some authorities use a comma to separate author's name from the title of the work and others use a full stop. In general, Americans recommend the full stop, but many English authorities prefer the comma. In the absence of a ruling from one's own institution, one may choose either form, but the important thing is that having chosen, one should stick to it. The same goes for publication details. Some prefer to retain the bracketed form as used in the footnotes, while others remove the brackets and separate the publishing details from the rest by using a full stop. Again, as for the footnotes, the publishing details may include or omit the name of the publisher. In setting out the complete Bibliography, it is normal practice to indent the second and subsequent lines of each entry. Examples will make clear the different possible forms.

Example of one entry under different forms

> Olivier, Laurence. *Confessions of an Actor.* London: Weidenfeld and Nicolson, 1982.
> Olivier, Laurence, *Confessions of an Actor* (London: Weidenfeld and Nicolson, 1982).

In each case, publishing details could be shortened, by the omission of the publisher's name, to London, 1982.

These, then, are the possible variations in format. I give below a list of examples of different kinds of entries, using the first form.

Examples of different kinds of entries

(1. A book by a single author.)

> Morris, Jan. *The Venetian Empire: A Sea Voyage.* London, 1980.

(2. A book by two authors.)

> Middlemass, Keith, and John Barnes. *Baldwin: A Biography.* London, 1969.

(*Note:* The name of the second author is not inverted, since it does not affect the alphabetical placing.)

(3. A book by several authors.)

> Parker, Geoffrey, and others. *The Thirty Years War.* London, 1984.

(4. An edition of an author's works.)

> Marvell, Andrew. *The Poems and Letters of Andrew Marvell,* ed. H. M. Margoliouth, 2 vols. 2nd edn Oxford, 1952.

(5. An anthology or edited collection.)

> Keating, Peter, ed. *The Victorian Prophets: A Reader from Carlyle to Wells.* Glasgow, 1981.

(6. A translation.)

> Virgil. *The Aeneid,* trans. W. F. Jackson Knight. Harmondsworth, 1956.

(7. An article in a journal.)

> Brittan, Samuel. 'Hayek, the New Right, and the Crisis of Social Democracy', *Encounter,* Vol. 54, No. 1 (January 1980), pp. 31–46.

(8. A chapter in an edited collection.)

> Vernon, M. D. 'Attention and Visual Perception', in *Readings in Psychology,* ed. John Cohen. London, 1964.

(9. An article in an encyclopedia.)

'Numismatics', *Encyclopedia Britannica*, vol. XV, pp. 615–34. 1964.

(10. A newspaper article.)

Chester, Lewis. 'The Truth about Beveridge', *Sunday Times*, 9 June 1985, p. 18.

(11. A pamphlet or guide.)

Guide to the British Museum. London, 1965.

(12. Material from the Internet.)

Barlow, Linda. (1999) *The Spider's Apprentice: A Helpful Guide to Web Search Engines* [Online], Monash Information Services. Available from: http://www.monash. com/spidap4.html [accessed 25 September 1999].

For further examples of footnotes and bibliographical entries, and the difference in form between them, the student is advised to study the Specimen Paper (Chapter 7).

Chapter 7

Specimen paper

This chapter consists of a paper written by an MA student and used with her permission. It illustrates most of the principles that have been outlined in this book, and provides illustrations of footnotes and Bibliography in practice. The length of this paper is naturally no guide to students, any more than the number of footnotes or bibliographical entries. These matters will be determined by the nature and requirements of each paper.

The paper was written using only printed sources. It has not seemed appropriate to update it. It is reproduced here as written, as an example of bibliography and footnotes from such sources, and as an example of the principles of shape and flow detailed above.

If the student were writing today much of the information gathering would have been via the Internet. I therefore discuss here some of the sites that might have been found.

When I tried this for the Fourth Edition I had difficulty in finding any sites with the words Nazi Propaganda. I had to use Nazi Propaganda + Goebbels. Things have certainly moved on since then. Using Google I found a large number of sites. The most important remains the German Propaganda Archive of Calvin College http://www.edu/academic/cas/gpa which contains a large collection of translations of Nazi propaganda speeches and writings, cartoons, posters, etc. All of these items of valuable primary source material can be accessed by hyperlinks. In addition there is a comprehensive bibliography for the subject with the most recent item dated 2002. The site also gives details of a forthcoming book *Bending Spines: The Propaganda of Nazi Germany and the German Democratic Republic* (Michigan State University Press, April 2004). One can hardly expect anything more up-to-date than that.

Another site with a great deal to offer, including a piece by Professor David Welch, is BBC – History – Nazi Propaganda. There was also material on Nazi Propaganda and Censorship.

Infoseek turned up results that were not found by Google. It reported 158,000 results for Nazi Propaganda and gave a base to search within results.

I also used Metasearch and found other sites. Through Alta Vista it yielded a new site *Real History and Dr. Joseph Goebbels*, with the facility to download an entire book by David Irving. The student by this time would probably be aware of the need to check reviews to see how controversial David Irving's views are.

The broad word search for Nazi Propaganda could be refined by adding concepts such as Film or Radio. I chose to use Nuremberg Rallies and found many other sites, including, with examples, how education was permeated with propaganda.

Clearly a student writing today would have an enormous amount of material, especially of a primary nature, to sift through and evaluate.

NAZI PROPAGANDA

BY

‒ ‒ ‒ ‒ ‒ ‒ ‒ ‒ ‒ ‒ ‒ ‒ ‒ ‒ ‒ ‒ ‒ ‒

Instructor . . . .

Course . . . .

Date . . . .

Abstract: Nazi Propaganda

Purpose: This paper examines the role of propaganda in the Nazi Party and government, its aims and methods, and some of the questions it raises.

Introduction: A general consideration of various definitions of propaganda and of its role in the Nazi success in Germany.

Section I: Nazi propaganda in the period of the Party's rise to power.

Section II: Nazi propaganda in the period from 1933 to the outbreak of war, when they had control of all the organs of the state.

Section III: Some questions and conclusions raised by a consideration of Nazi propaganda.

NAZI PROPAGANDA

Introduction

Propaganda is so central to the Nazi system that it is hardly possible to talk of that system without the word cropping up in the first few sentences. When we ask how did this movement get a grip on a great, cultured European nation, it is all too easy to reply at once 'Propaganda'. But is it really as simple as that? It is the intention of this paper to examine the aims and methods of Nazi Propaganda and then, in the light of this examination, to consider certain fundamental questions it raises.

First, it is necessary to consider what propaganda is. Propaganda has existed from time immemorial in an unsystematic sense embracing the various means by which governments from ancient times have succeeded in riveting the allegiance of the governed. The word itself is of comparatively recent origin. The *Oxford English Dictionary* gives its derivation from an association of the Roman Catholic Church *de propaganda fide* for propagating the faith. The first usage quoted is in 1842 when it is said to be 'applied in modern political language as a term of reproach to secret associations for the spread of opinions and principles which are viewed by most governments with horror and aversion'. Thus already it had acquired the pejorative sense which was to cling to it. The O.E.D., however, is studiously neutral in its own definition: 'Any association, systematic scheme, or concerted movement for the propagation of a particular doctrine or practice.'

But, if propaganda has a long history, it is generally acknowledged that propaganda as we think of it is the creation of the twentieth century. It required certain conditions for its successful application which only the twentieth century has produced: the industrial and urban society which draws large numbers of people together, at the same time as it shatters old stable relationships and fragments society; mass literacy; and the technical means of mass communication and suggestion. It can be no coincidence that totalitarian regimes have built on these conditions propaganda machines of immense success. The Nazi system was the first to use all modern means of communication to the full, to elevate propaganda into a science in itself, based on the sciences of sociology and psychology, and to convert the entire machinery of social and cultural life into one vast propaganda machine. 'Propaganda is an inalienable and vital function of the modern state', Goebbels declared.[1] As such it achieved a considerable success, at least as far as the Hitler cult was concerned. It has been many times remarked that the regime was overthrown in the end by external war, not by internal strains or revolution.[2] Indeed, a study showed that from June 1944 to April 1945 more than 60% of German soldiers retained their faith in Hitler. Moreover, despite the fact that in the last four months of the war communications were cut off, and police and party pressures were sporadic, resistance to the allies continued, and there was none of the internal collapse of 1918, showing that the people had been 'propagandised in depth'.[3]

It would perhaps be useful here to examine another definition of propaganda which takes these twentieth-century characteristics into account. Jacques Ellul, in his perceptive study *Propaganda*, gives this definition which he qualifies as only partial: 'propaganda is a set of methods employed by an organized group that wants to bring about the active or passive participation in its actions of a mass of individuals, psychologically unified through psychological manipulations and incorporated in an organization'.[4] This is a much better working definition when one is examining Nazi propaganda. It has been enlarged to include not only opinions but actions, and it conveys the ideas of the psychological, or irrational, means, and of the psychologically unified mass which are so central to its success. Goebbels wrote of the Ministry for Popular Enlightenment and Propaganda, 'I see the first task of this new ministry as establishing a coordination between the Government and the whole people.'[5] The effects of this, and the methods used, will be examined more fully in Section II below.

It is possible to distinguish three stages in Nazi propaganda: first its use in their rise to power from tiny beginnings to that of an important minority party; second its use when they had control of government, and therefore the organs to impose their will fully; and third when they were at war. Since the problems of war propaganda are much the same for all countries and the Nazis were less innovative in that respect, I propose to confine myself in this paper to the first two. In the first period the seeds of most of the later

Nazi propaganda methods were sown, but they required control of all the organs of the state to come to full fruition.

Section I: The Propaganda of the Minority Party

It is impossible in reading *Mein Kampf*[6] not to be amazed at the conscious, sure, developed grasp of mass manipulation which it reveals, all the more amazing when one considers that Volume I was published in 1925 and Volume II in 1926. It is on this that much of Hitler's reputation for 'political genius' rests. A quite disproportionate amount of the book is given to an exposition of propaganda methods; he reverts to it over and over again, showing the depth of his interest, and many of what might be called his more political ideas seem shaped to propaganda ends, a point to which I shall return at the end of this paper. Moreover, it is these sections of the book which have most vitality. As Alan Bullock puts it, they 'stand out in brilliant contrast with the turgid attempts to explain his entirely unoriginal ideas'.[7] Hitler gives a detailed exposition of the methods to be followed, but at its heart lie two interconnected principles: the appeal was to be to the broad masses, and, for this reason, it was to be to the emotions, to the irrational element, and not to the intellect. Because the appeal was to be to the masses it was to be simplified and expressed in very black and white terms, with constant 'As soon as our own propaganda admits so much as a glimmer of right on the other side, the foundation for doubt in our own right has been laid' (p. 183): 'the art of all truly great national leaders ... consists ... in not dividing the attention of a people, but in concentrating it upon a single foe ... It belongs to the genius of a great leader to make even adversaries far removed from one another seem to belong to the same category ... Once the wavering mass sees itself in a struggle against too many enemies objectivity will put in an appearance ...' (p. 118). 'Faith is harder to shake than knowledge, love succumbs less to change than respect, hate is more enduring than aversion ... Anyone who wants to win the broad masses must know the key that opens the door to their heart. Its name is not objectivity (read weakness) but will and power' (pp. 337–8).

In achieving this appeal to the emotions rather than the intellect Hitler relied upon 'the magic power of the spoken word ... the firebrand of the word ... a storm of hot passion' (p. 107), of which he himself was a consummate master, and which he felt was self-correcting in a way that the written word addressed to impersonal and unknown readers would never be. The speaker 'will always let himself be borne by the great masses in such a way that instinctively the very words come to his lips that he needs to speak to the hearts of the audience. And if he errs, even in the slightest, he has a living correction before him' (p. 470). How accomplished he was in this respect has been asserted by Otto Strasser: 'Hitler responds to the vibrations of the human heart with the delicacy of a seismograph . . . Adolf Hitler enters a hall. He sniffs the air. For a minute he gropes, feels his way, senses the atmosphere. Suddenly he bursts forth. His words go like an arrow to their target, he touches each private wound on the raw, liberating the mass unconscious, expressing its innermost aspirations, telling it what it most wants to hear.'[8] It is interesting in this regard to notice that, while the radio was used by Hitler to great effect, he made few live broadcasts but relied instead on recordings of speeches actually delivered, where he could secure the response of a live audience.[9]

Hitler deliberately directed his appeal to the emotions, including that of physical terror. It has been many times pointed out that Nazism bears all the marks of a perverted religion, a religion of hate, not love, with the 'rhetoric of hell', and with all the symbolism of religion,[10] and Hitler admits to having borrowed from the Roman Catholic Church with its mysterious twilight, burning lamps, incense, etc. He was to use these devices in his mass meetings, to be held at night when the power to resist a stronger will is lowered. Hitler saw in his mass meetings the key to winning over the fragmented individual by incorporating him or her into an immensely strong whole. His metaphors for this are extraordinarily vivid:

> The gigantic demonstrations, these parades of hundreds of thousands of men, which burned into the small wretched individual the proud conviction that, paltry worm as he was, he was nevertheless a part of the great dragon, beneath whose burning breath the hated bourgeois world would some day go up in fire and flame and the proletarian dictatorship would celebrate its ultimate final victory. (p. 473)

> When from his little workshop or big factory, in which he feels very small, he steps for the first time into a mass meeting and has thousands of people of the same opinions around him . . . The will, the longing and also the power of thousands are

accumulated in every individual. The man who enters such a meeting doubting and wavering leaves it inwardly reinforced. He has become a link with the community. (p. 479)

To reinforce this sense of community Hitler used participation to the full. The Labour Service units, and others at the rallies, were trained in choric speaking, and the many collections of documents on Nazism offer repeated evidence of the infectious enthusiasm conveyed by the refrain of Sieg Heil.[11]

Hitler also had great faith in the emotional power of symbolism. He described the effect on him of seeing in a pre-war Marxist meeting 'the suggestive magic of spectacle', 'a sea of red flags, red scarves and red flowers' (p. 492). He himself adopted the swastika as a symbol, and designed the red, black and white flag incorporating it, and the standards which were to be potent symbols of Nazism.

Thus, by 1925, Hitler, who had been appointed in 1920 to direct the propaganda of the infant party, had already shown a firm grasp of the essentials he was to use. In that year he first met Dr. Joseph Goebbels, the other great master of propaganda, and almost his equal in oratory. In the following year Goebbels was made Gauleiter of Berlin and began to develop the methods of propaganda which were to help the Nazis to electoral successes in the Depression period. In 1930 he was appointed to head the central Propaganda Department in the Party H.Q. at Munich.

All the elements were there, though for the present they could be used in only a limited way. The party had a network of local organizations and its own press. Its national newspaper, the *Völkischer Beobachter*, became a daily paper in 1923. In 1929 its circulation was only 18,400. With the Depression there was a big growth to 128,000 in 1931, but its circulation became large only with the Nazi assumption of power. In 1932 the Nazi press consisted of 59 daily journals, but their combined circulation was only about three-quarters of a million.[12] Many of them were 'violent in language . . . crude almost beyond belief. The worst of them scarcely resembled a weekly newspaper but rather a badly printed brochure of ten to twenty pages filled with the wildest and meanest diatribes.'[13] But, bad as they were, they served as party organs and disseminators of party propaganda. At election times their print order was increased and many were distributed free.[14]

The uniforms of the S.A. men, the swastika symbol, the flags, the military parades and constant meetings utilized the military spirit and created a feeling of omnipresence, and of greater numbers than the movement could actually claim.[15] Goebbels early realized the importance of what he called 'the conquest of the streets'. In the new mass age the street was 'the criterion of modern politics. He who can conquer the streets can also conquer the masses.'[16] Thus meetings were announced and held in a deliberately provocative manner to encourage street brawls and violence. By this means several objects were achieved: physical terror was used, as Hitler had advocated; the Nazis presented themselves as numerous, vigorous and activist; and politics became irrationalized.[17]

In organizing their meetings the Nazis showed particular skill in appealing to sectional and economic interests. They created smaller organizations for occupational groups, the members of which were able to propagandize their colleagues. They also exploited local issues and interests. In W. S. Allen's 'Thalburg' (the name he gave, for reasons of confidentiality, to the small town in Germany of which he had done a thorough study), with its high proportion of government employees, they announced a meeting on 'Civil Service and National Socialism', and held other meetings devoted to the interests of artisans, businessmen, civil servants, pensioners and workmen.[18]

Though they were not yet able to make that thorough assault on youth and education that governmental power made possible, the Nazis had made a beginning there also. The Hitler Youth was founded in 1926, though by 1932 its total enrolment was only 107,956, as compared with about ten million in other youth organizations.[19] But the small numbers somewhat belie the potentiality for influence of the movement. A youth described his reasons for joining in 1930 thus: 'I wanted to be in a boys' club where I could strive towards a nationalistic ideal. The Hitler youth had camping, hikes, and group meetings . . . There were no social or class distinctions . . . We weren't fully conscious of what we were doing but we enjoyed ourselves and also felt important.'[20] The potential menace of the movement was felt by those concerned with the growth of Nazism in the Protestant Youth movement: 'certainly 70% of our young people, often lacking knowledge of the facts are in ardent sympathy'. 'Fifth formers are not really much concerned with the study of Hitler's thoughts; it is simply something irrational, something infectious that makes the blood pulse through one's veins and conveys an impression that something great is under way.' A complaint of 1930 in Oldenburg of Hitler Youth intimidating other pupils in the school goes on to reveal that many of the teachers are National Socialists or sympathizers and cannot be relied on to stop it. 'The relationship of trust necessary between teachers and parents and their children has completely gone.'[21]

In all this building up of specialist groups, business, youth, etc., the Nazis foreshadowed their later takeover of all clubs and associations in Germany.

As with the Press so with the other mass media, the Nazis were able to make only limited use of them. Goebbels had an imaginative grasp of the potentiality of the mass media. The originality of his concepts can be shown by two examples. The first is his very 'modern' campaign of a sequence of three posters for his paper *Der Angriff* (*The Attack*):

The Attack?
The attack takes place on July 4th.

And finally, when curiosity had been fully aroused, the announcement that *The Attack* was a new German Monday newspaper.

The second example is his ingenious use of recording. In the 1932 campaign, he had challenged Chancellor Brüning to appear for a public debate on the same platform with him. On his refusal, Goebbels had one of his radio speeches recorded and played it, with frequent interruptions for himself to challenge or question his invisible and 'speechless' opponent. 'The public was in a rage of enthusiasm.'[22] This gives some idea of what Goebbels might have done with the government controlled radio, if at his disposal in those early years. Goebbels also realized the power of film for propaganda, but in the early years the party's tiny film unit could make only amateurish films for private showing at party meetings, and shared with other parties the advantage of having its mass rallies featured occasionally in the news reels.

With Hitler's highly developed sense of the importance of the spectacle, pageantry, ritual and the mass meeting, it is not surprising that the Nuremberg rallies were an early development. The first party rally was held in Munich in 1923, and from the beginning much of the ceremonial of the ritual consecration of the flags and the march past was established. From then on, including a second one in the same year, rallies were held mainly in Nuremberg, chosen as symbolic of the Nazi fusion of past and present. Nuremberg was a medieval city in pure German style, associated with Dürer and other German artists, and made famous by its rediscovery during the German Romantic Movement. It was heavily publicized by the Nazis in a big propaganda campaign in newspapers and magazines. Further rallies were held in 1926, 1927 and 1929. Membership of the Party rose from 17,000 in 1926 to 40,000 in 1927, and the rally of 1927 was the first big demonstration of its strength. Hitler took the salute at a torchlight procession of about 30,000 brownshirts, and it is estimated that 160,000 people attended the rally.[23]

In the 1932 election campaign, with the acquisition of more funds, the Nazi propaganda machine showed what it could do. Even the smallest villages were canvassed. Films of Hitler and Goebbels were made and shown. 50,000 gramophone records were distributed by Goebbels' Department and use was made of recorded speeches played by loudspeaker vans, as a substitute for the radio which they did not control. But the greatest effort, as might be expected from Hitler's belief in the power of the spoken word, responsive to the living audience, was put into mass meetings, in which the Nazi orators stirred the people to frenzied enthusiasm. Goebbels made nineteen speeches in Berlin, besides those he made in other towns, while Hitler addressed audiences of up to 100,000, taking advantage of the microphones which had become standard equipment at Nazi meetings from 1930.[24]

Despite all this effort Hitler's vote was only 11 million to Hindenburg's 18 million, and in Berlin he came third. Hindenburg did not secure the necessary absolute majority, however, and another election had to be held. Here Goebbels showed his ingenuity in propaganda when he used the device of having Hitler travel across Germany by plane with the inspiring slogan 'Hitler over Germany'. This had several effects: Hitler spoke directly to about a million people; he took advantage of the public interest in the novelty of aviation, creating interest and enthusiasm by speaking in three of four widely separated cities on the same day; and he utilized the almost mythic effect of arrival by air.[25] Goebbels' superb press organization took full advantage of this, especially the fortuitous fact that Hitler's plane took off for Düsseldorf in a violent storm when all other air traffic was grounded. This episode was later used to great effect in a propaganda school text.[26]

By these ingenious means, and the sheer sustained effort of their campaign, they pushed Hitler's vote up another 2 million, though Hindenburg with 19 million easily obtained his absolute majority. In the other elections of 1932 the Nazi Party kept up its pressure.

In July, in his third flight over Germany, Hitler visited fifty towns. Bullock gives the figures for his share of the vote as rising from 30% in March to 37.3% in July, and falling to 33.1% in November, with a drop of 40%, from the July figure, in a later local election in Thuringia.[27] This is the strongest argument for a belief that in a fair field with no favour, Nazi propaganda was not enough, that with the Depression lessening and the particular constellation of events which had led to their big increase in support dying away, they had 'peaked' already.

Section II: The Propaganda of Government

The appointment of Hitler as Chancellor in 1933 was to give the Nazis the full power of the State to create a new system of total propaganda. 'Nazi ideology tried to claim the whole man – in his political, economic, social and even private life. Propaganda therefore had the function of creating a "new" man and a "new" society.'[28] Now at last Hitler had the opportunity to abolish the dreaded 'objectivity', to ensure that all voices were silenced, save one, and that a cultural and intellectual wall was built round Germany within which only an approved set of ideas flourished.

Goebbels was made head of the Ministry of Popular Enlightenment and Propaganda, whose work was subdivided into many departments, but unified by its total scope and one-man control. The number of divisions varied, growing to fourteen by 1942, but an idea of their all-embracing quality can be gathered from this list for 1936:

> **Division I**: Legislation and legal problems; Budget, Finances, and Accounting; Personnel Administration; Ministerial Library; National Chamber of Culture; Council of Commercial Advertising; Fairs and Expositions.

> **Division II**: Coordination of Popular Enlightenment and Propaganda; Regional Agencies of the Ministry; German Academy of Politics; Official Ceremonies and Demonstrations; National Emblems; Racial Questions; Treaty of Versailles; National Literature and Publishing; Opposing Ideologies; Youth Organization; Business and Social Politics; Public Health and Athletics; Eastern and Border Questions; National Travel Committee.

Division III: Radio; National Broadcasting Company.

Division IV: National and Foreign Press; Journalism; Press Archives; News Service; National Association of the German Press.

Division V: Cinema; Moving Picture Industry; Cinema Censorship; Youth Literature Censorship.

Division VI: Theatre, Music, and Art; Theatre Management; Stage Direction; Design; Folk Art.

Division VII: Protection against Counter-Propaganda at Home and Abroad.[29]

I have reproduced this somewhat lengthy list because it illustrates clearly the determination of the propagandists to leave no channel unfilled with their propaganda, nor free for anyone else's ideas. The list is nothing if not exhaustive.

Swiftly the State secured total control of the mass media. The Nazis secured a totally subservient press by a number of steps. First, in 1933, they closed down Socialist and Communist papers, confiscating their plant, and took over the Reich Association of the German Press. All journalists and editors were required to belong to it and screened for 'racial and political reliability'.[30] The Editors Law of 1933 made the editors quasi-state officials, responsible for the content of their papers while the publishers became mere business managers. Clear directives were issued to the Press and were secret and absolutely binding. In 1933 and 1934 the Nazi papers were brought under the Nazi publishing house Eher Verlag, under the Reich Leader for the Party Press, Max Amann. But this was not enough: the papers with a heavy national circulation were still privately owned. At the end of 1934 the party-owned papers had barely 25% of total circulation.[31] The Nazi attitude is revealed in this memorandum:

> The National Socialist *Weltanschauung* demands total acceptance and does not tolerate the propagation of other basic ideas. On this basis a state whose foundation is the National Socialist movement recognizes only a National Socialist Press.[32]

Thus in 1935 the Amann Decrees, of very comprehensive scope, struck at all trade and religious papers; all papers in areas where there was too much competition; and all produced by corporations, or persons with major interests outside the publishing field, in effect all the big newspaper chains. In the next eighteen months 500 or 600 papers disappeared or merged. By 1939 the party-owned and controlled press held about two-thirds of the total circulation, the 2,000 privately owned papers the other one-third.[33] Even within this framework the Nazis secured tighter control through the Reich Press Chief, Otto Dietrich. Daily, or twice daily, the editors were called to a Press Conference where they were handed '10 or 12 closely typed pages, containing many prohibitions and few permissions. It prescribed the treatment of the specified themes with regard to space, tone, headlines, and placement down to the last detail.' Even the words to be used were prescribed: 'From 1933 onwards editors became more and more rubber stamps for officially stated views.'[34]

Amann said the editors complained they received a one-inch file of news and a three-inch file of directives.[35] Under the circumstances circulation dropped and Goebbels was continually calling for the more imaginative treatment and more originality needed to raise it, which his own self-defeating policy prevented. He complained in 1936 of those who stopped buying a paper: 'These people are not now reached by any newspaper and have therefore been quite inadequately influenced by the state and the party.'[36] But despite a big advertising campaign he could not win them back until the war created a demand for news and hence rising circulation. This illustrates a recurring difficulty of the Ministry of Propaganda: the State might control the media but how far could it force people to absorb unpalatable material? This is a point to which I shall return in the final section of the paper.

It was otherwise, however, with radio. Here the Nazi control was effective. It was already well set up to take over since, in 1926, the Ministry of Posts held 51% of the stock of the National Broadcasting Company and there was a supervisory committee of three to scrutinize programme content. By the end of 1933 all provincial radio companies were dissolved and the national government had taken over all radio facilities.[37] Moreover, it put pressure on manufacturers to produce cheap sets. By the beginning of the war a set was produced for under £3 and it was estimated that 70% of households had one. The cheap set in Germany was deliberately designed to pick up only German stations.[38] Lest even the remaining segment of the population should escape, or those with sets exercise their privilege of failing to listen, an elaborate system of wireless wardens was set up.

> It is the duty of these men to organise reception; they must see that every school and public square, coffee house, theatre and factory is fitted with receivers and amplifiers which make community reception possible. At times of important broadcasts, all work is stopped. Shops are closed. The flow of traffic, which might cause interference, ceases. It has been estimated that about 75% of the population hears the official transmission upon such occasions.[39]

This captive audience was offered programming carefully planned to foster National Socialist ideas. From overt propaganda in the sense of direct speeches, government proclamations, talks on history from the Nazi point of view or on racial doctrines, through lectures on military subjects and military music, to folklore, German music and glowing descriptions of the German countryside, nothing was neglected that would build up the right world view. Programming was even carefully synchronized with workers' lunch and break times in factories, and the wireless wardens were to forward listener response. Care was taken to use the medium for the maximum effect. In 1933 Hitler spoke to the nation for 45 minutes from the Siemens electric plant, standing on a dynamo, surrounded by workers, heralded by shrieking sirens and the roar of machinery.[40] There was an even more impressive use of sound effects in a broadcast from Nuremberg in September 1938.

> On a foundation of Wagnerian music there was heard a daunting rumbling, slow and emphatic of drums, and heavy footfalls pounding the earth, together with an indescribable rattle and swish and pant of armed masses on the march. This noise, now growing, now receding, must have clutched at the hearts of the millions of listeners, filling them with apprehension of disaster – a feeling of fascination and fear, deliberately produced by the men who staged the spectacle ... This was 100 per cent Hitlerist propaganda, an attempt to intimidate, to subject the millions of listeners in the world to psychical violation.[41]

This is a far cry indeed from the fireside chats of Roosevelt, and the low-key discourses of Baldwin, pipe in hand.

It is worth spending a little time on radio because this was the method *par excellence* by which the Nazi regime reached the masses.[42] It was the nearest Hitler could get to making the whole nation the audience for his 'magic power of the spoken word',[43] and by the method I have outlined above, of broadcasting speeches delivered before live audiences, he could still secure the 'living correction' of the live audience. The audiences for Hitler's big speeches have been variously estimated at from 56 to 80 million, including, of course, some from outside Germany.

The Nazis also controlled the film industry. In 1933 the Aryan clause banned Jews from any part of the industry and some of the best artists began to emigrate. In 1934 only members of the *Reichsfilmkammer* were allowed to produce films and there was an all-inclusive censorship decree. At the same time foreign films with Jewish artists were banned, as were those with unacceptable content. Censorship was interpreted in the narrowest possible way, since not only what was unacceptable in terms of political and ideological content was disallowed, but also anything which went against the narrow and somewhat old-fashioned morality of the Nazi view. In the circumstances it is not surprising that the German film industry declined and its non-propaganda products became empty of content and essentially escapist. Only a small number of strictly propaganda films was made, since the German people had to be induced to pay to go to the cinema and showed a lack of desire to see propaganda films. 'Goebbels believed that propaganda was most effective when it was insidious, when its message was concealed within the framework of popular entertainment.'[44] But this proved difficult to achieve. It proved more successful to rely on short films and newsreels for propaganda, and to use the pulling power of the feature film. To ensure a captive audience after 1941 it was common practice to lock the doors of the cinema during the showing of newsreels.[45] Of about 1,363 feature films under the Third Reich, 208 were banned after the war by various Allied Governments for containing propaganda, many of them on rather slight grounds.[46] The most successful propagandist film maker, who combined entertainment with a strong propagandist line, urging sacrifice for country, or denigrating democracy, was Karl Ritter. He declared, 'I want to show German youth that senseless, sacrificial death has its moral value', and it is estimated that about six million boys were exposed to his films between 1936 and 1939.[47] The most notorious combined entertainment and propaganda film was *Jud Süss* which came out in 1940 and was a great box office success. It was designed to foster anti-Semitism. It catered for degraded tastes, with rape and torture sequences, and its showing in Vienna was followed by the trampling to death of an elderly Jew on a public street, by a Hitler Youth band who had seen the film.[48]

Best known of the propaganda films are *Triumph of the Will* (1935) and *Olympia* (1938) by Leni Riefenstahl. Controversy still rages over these, with conflicting views of their artistry and ideological content, and a back-handed tribute to the power of the first is provided by opposition to its showing. As a piece of education in the technique and content of Nazi propaganda it can hardly be surpassed. It was meant as a showcase of the Nuremberg rally, both at home and abroad. In effect, it was to do visually what the radio could do aurally. Nevertheless, despite, or perhaps because of, its artistry, it was not a box office success. It seems to have had limited appeal and a condensed version about one-third of the original length was usually shown. Moreover, though it won a prize in France, only a few countries abroad friendly to Germany showed it.[49]

These are the obvious mass media used to spread Nazi propaganda, but the range of the Propaganda Ministry's activity, as shown above, indicates how widely it pervaded every aspect of cultural and intellectual life. Censorship applied not only to the press and film but also to the stage and literature. There were book burnings and purgings of libraries. The Nazis had their official art, very representational, in which nature, peasant and family motifs abounded. They castigated all else, for example in the exhibitions of Degenerate Art. Even the applied arts were used to spread the Nazi message. Propaganda pervaded every aspect of public and private life.

Above all they were anxious that no individual should find support and cohesion in any group not permeated with their spirit. To this end, they broke up or took over all other clubs and associations, whether economic, business, trade union, religious, special interest or purely social. This process as it affected one German town is vividly described by W. S. Allen in a chapter which he aptly calls 'The Atomization of Society'. He concludes:

> Thus by the summer of 1933, the Nazis had either broken up, altered, fused, or brought under control most of the clubs and societies of Thalburg. The complex and diversified social

organization of the town had been almost completely uprooted. In most cases the Nazis tried to fill the vacuum, but often people stopped coming altogether ... What social life there was continued in the most basic gatherings: the *Stammtisch*, the beer-and-cards evenings, or small social gatherings in homes. Even these were threatened as people began to distrust one another. What was the value of getting together with others to talk if you had to be careful about what you said? Thus to a great extent the individual was atomized. By the process of *Gleichschaltung* [variously translated as standardization, or putting everything in the same gear] individuals had no choice: solitude or mass relationships via some Nazi organization.[50]

Mention has already been made of one of the earliest organizations which the Nazis intended to act as replacements: the Hitler Youth. Like all dictators, Hitler set great store by capturing the next generation. In a speech on 6 November 1933 he said: 'When an opponent declares, "I will not come over to your side", I calmly say, "Your child belongs to us already ... What are you? You will pass on. Your descendants, however, now stand in the new camp. In a short time, they will know nothing but this community."'[51] Obviously Nazi propaganda permeated the educational system totally, but they also took over most of the out of school hours of youth as well. As we have seen above, there was a natural appeal to youth in the movement, but even so, at the beginning of 1933 it had only 1% of the total membership of youth organizations in the country. At first pressure was used to make others join, but in December 1936 all German Youth had to join.[52] This captive membership was then thoroughly propagandized. After 1934 a monthly Film Hour was mandatory in all groups.[53] The programme for a fortnight's camp,[54] with its daily patriotic password, propagandist motto, and ideological discussion subject for the community hour, shows how they were saturated with propaganda.

The other movement which drew vast numbers of workers was 'Strength Through Joy', created in 1933 to help the worker to use leisure hours profitably. It concerned itself with securing attendance at lectures, concerts, theatres, opera and sports activities. It operated travel schemes, enabling workers to spend holidays abroad, and even made plans for the Volkswagen, the people's car. It was also closely associated with radio programming of a cultural and uplifting nature.

Finally, in this necessarily incomplete survey of propaganda methods, there was the greatest showcase of all, both for domestic and foreign audiences: the Nuremberg Rallies. These, where all Hitler's propaganda ideas from *Mein Kampf* could be brought into play, became ever more grandiose. As soon as the Nazis seized power Hitler began the building of a colossal permanent setting for the rallies, which was intended to become the centre of the cultic tradition of the Thousand Year Reich. Building continued even into the war, and it was so dear to Hitler's heart that it was not stopped until 1943. Everything was planned to be on a massive scale, the site covering an area of 16.5 square kilometres. The military parade ground was to seat 160,000, and to have a platform for important visitors, crowned with a sculpture 46 feet higher than the Statue of Liberty. A huge stadium was planned which would seat 400,000 spectators.[55] Hitler justified this grandiose conception thus, in a speech in 1939: 'I do this to restore to each individual German his self-respect. In a hundred areas I want to say to the individual: we are not inferior; on the contrary we are the complete equal of every other nation.'[56]

Every rally was conceived in stage and operatic terms, as is shown by the system of markers on the parade ground for the exact distribution of the 8,000 banners; the enormous number of spotlights and klieg lights; and the control panel of coloured lights Hitler had in front of him.[57] *Triumph of the Will* gives a clear idea of the massed power, the sense of solidarity, and the quasi-religious feeling that could be induced by the events of these rallies. Lest this should be seen as the distorting lens of Leni Riefenstahl, I will quote two more neutral accounts of the powerful impact the rallies made. The *New York Times* reporter wrote:

As he [Hitler] appeared there shone upward from a hidden circle of 150 army searchlights behind the grandstands as many spears of light to the central point above. It was the same device employed at the closing ceremony of the Olympic Games but it was greatly improved and enlarged . . . Then suddenly there appeared in the distance a mass of advancing red colour. It was the 25,000 banners of Nazi organizations from all parts of Germany . . . there was presented a spectacle of a great tide of crimson seeping through the lanes between the solid blocs of brown. Simultaneously the minor searchlights along the pillared rim above the grandstands were turned down on the field, lighting up the gilded eagles on the standards, so the flood of red was flecked with gold. The effect was indescribably beautiful.[58]

The second quotation is from Sir Neville Henderson, the British Ambassador to Germany, who described a Nuremberg rally thus: 'I had spent six years in St. Petersburg before the war in the best days of the old Russian ballet but for grandiose beauty I have never seen a ballet to compare with it.'[59]

Above all the rallies were participatory functions with choric speaking to enhance the sense of solidarity, and fervid shouts of Sieg Heil. The *New York Times* reporter recounts the extraordinary effect produced when the closing ceremony was relayed to a hotel lounge filled with working journalists, from foreign countries and, one would have thought, hard-bitten and resistant:

As the cheers from the hall following the 'Sieg Heil' with which he concluded died away, the hotel audience to a man and woman rose to its feet with arms raised in the Nazi salute and joined in the emotional singing of 'Deutschland' followed by the 'Horst Wessel Lied'. It was typical of eight days of steadily mounting excitement that words fail adequately to describe.[60]

This massed power and mounting excitement were conveyed across Germany and the world by radio, film and press.

Section III: Some Questions and Conclusions

Such were the main outlines of the propaganda system created by the Nazis. Apart from viewing it with awe and horror, we have, I think, by way of conclusion, to consider three inter-related questions. How far could it succeed against the people's will, and therefore what was the extent of its success? Was it a means or an end? Did it contain the seeds of its own destruction? These are large questions which can only be touched on briefly here.

To start with the first question, it is obvious that the propagandees must place themselves in a position to be receptive: they must look at the poster; buy and read the papers; attend the cinema or meeting; switch on and listen to the radio. As we have seen above, the propaganda machine did everything it could to ensure that they had no choice. This was particularly true of the use of radio and of the indoctrination of children at school and youth organizations. But even more, the propagandees must be psychologically receptive to the ideas presented. Goebbels realized this when he was careful to ensure that specific propaganda was directed to specific groups, and Hitler even more so when he spoke of the 'living corrective' of the audience. To some extent they were drawing out what was already there. Albert Speer, in looking back on his own first experience of Hitler's speeches, writes, 'As I see it today, these politicians in particular were in fact moulded by the mob itself, guided by its yearnings and its daydreams . . . Certainly the masses roared to the beat set by Hitler's and Goebbels's baton; yet they were not the true conductors. The mob determined the theme.'[61] A recent German writer has described propaganda as 'not only a means of manipulation but an indicator of what people sincerely hoped to be true'.[62] A similar view is taken by Jacques Ellul, who, in denying that the process of propagandizing involves an active (evil) element and a passive (victim) element, describes it as 'a sociological phenomenon in the sense that it has roots and reasons in the needs of the group that will sustain it'.[63]

There can be no denying that many Germans of this period craved leadership, authority, a sense of direction, a strong nationalist, and even militarist, government. Many people felt the attraction of a movement which called for a sense of sacrifice and offered them through this, and through commitment to what seemed a larger cause, a chance of reintegration into a community, and, supposedly, a classless community. Nazi propaganda could build on all these desires. It could build on patriotism, on the desire to be recognized as a great Power again, and to remove the humiliating features of the Treaty of Versailles. Ian Kershaw, in his challenge to the accepted view of the success of Nazi propaganda, distinguishes areas where propaganda could build on accepted values from those where a consensus had to be manufactured, or hostile counterprevailing forces existed. He finds the chief success in the first category.[64] These accepted values, which I have listed above, coalesced in the creation of the Führer Myth, in the success of which as a unifying principle in the state, Goebbels took much pride. Significantly, as was pointed out at the beginning of this paper, this myth held to the end of the war, long past when reality should have destroyed it. The Führer was presented as above politics, and as personally responsible for the achievements of the 1930s, which had done so much to restore German pride. Up to

1939 propaganda operated against a background of considerable success: there was a series of achievements gained without bloodshed. And this is a significant point: the Führer was presented as a man of peace. The whole tenor of Nazi propaganda glorified war and was designed to prepare the nation for war, but in this it did not succeed. There were no cheering crowds for war in 1939, as there had been in 1914.

The same qualification holds good with regard to anti-Semitism: it was difficult for propaganda to succeed where people had personal knowledge of Jewish people. Kershaw considers the greatest success of propaganda in this field to be in persuading people that there was a Jewish question, and in depersonalizing the Jews, but that terror and legal discrimination, not propaganda, were behind the exclusion of Jews.[65] A recent study of a small town in Germany records numerous small acts of kindness to Jews, and would bear out the difficulty of propagandizing people whose personal experience contradicted the propaganda.[66] The Nazis tried to use propaganda 'as a tool to destroy the disturbing independence of reality',[67] but without entire success. They did not have enough time to see if their methods would have worked in the vacuum they tried to create for the younger generation, as suggested in Hitler's speech quoted above. But many of the soldiers who continued the hopeless fight must have been indoctrinated through the Hitler Youth. On the evidence above we must conclude that the propaganda machine was most successful where it articulated desires already present, where the people willed their own fate, though without fully understanding what they willed.

This brings us to the second question: was propaganda a means or an end? It is hard to read *Mein Kampf* without feeling that there is a blurring of distinction between the two. There is so little ideological content in this book. It is mainly a diatribe of hate and destruction with the only positive concept that of power, essentially for its own sake. Even the few ideas seem shaped to the propaganda methods that are so vividly described. Did Hitler's obsessive hatred of the Jews lead him to see their hand everywhere, or was it his propaganda concept of the single foe? Did he really believe in the nation as community, or was this his way of winning the masses? It is difficult to see anything in this work but a total disregard of people, as such, and a total glorification of power. Every aspect of the propaganda machine that this paper has examined seems ultimately devoid of positive content but, rather, imbued with nihilism. In a telling phrase Allen speaks of 'a ritual devoid of inner content'.[68] Ellul has again pinpointed this aspect of modern propaganda. Lenin and Hitler, he says, were responsible for a great innovation.

> It was to understand that the modern world is essentially a world of means . . . This completely transformed the relations between ideology and propaganda . . . Propaganda then became the major fact; with respect to it, ideologies became mere epiphenomena . . . Some will object that the great movements that have used propaganda, such as Communism or Nazism, did have a doctrine and did create an ideology. I reply that this was not their principal object: ideology and doctrine were merely accessories used by propaganda to mobilize individuals. The aim was the power of the party or State, supported by the masses.[69]

Certainly the evidence marshalled above would suggest no fixed body of doctrine, but rather the determination to articulate the desires of as many as possible, so as to secure the integration of the individual in the State, and thus a readiness for whatever policy the State wished to carry out.

Finally, the third question: did Nazi propaganda contain the seeds of its own destruction? I have suggested above that it was self-defeating in many of its forms. People ceased to buy papers; films lost money; social organizations withered; standardization struck at the cultural life of the nation, which, if there was any point in the glorification of the Volk, should have been flourishing. One could add that it is considered the grip on ideas and education set back German science and thus contributed to eventual defeat in the war. Moreover, the central concept of the cult, and the one it was most successful in projecting, the leadership principle, was itself self-defeating. The Führer myth, projecting Hitler as the Saviour sent by God to Germany, was constantly emphasized in every aspect of propaganda.[70] This image, built on early successes, inevitably called for continuing successes to sustain it, and thus encouraged the tendency already present to take greater and greater risks, and to pursue a more and more adventurous policy. This need for constant success had other effects, it has been suggested, in making Hitler reluctant to move too far in the direction of a war economy, when war came. He opposed rationing, and taxes remained relatively low.

'German output of consumer goods was hardly dented by the war, between 1939 and 1942.'[71] Thus, again, the needs of propaganda hampered the success of the very objective it was designed to serve. Moreover, the creation of the Führer myth fostered an impression of infallibility, isolating Hitler more and more from any point of view but his own. The frenzy of the crowds at meetings ended in Hitler hypnotizing himself. 'The irrational adulation and deification of Hitler demonstrated during this hysterical week [Nuremberg Party rally, 1934] increased Hitler's megalomania; he felt that he could now whip the German masses into any frenzy, that they would carry out any order he might give them.'[72] When there were no successes to build on, and this reaction was less likely to sustain him, Hitler withdrew from the public eye,[73] listened less and less to advice and became more and more divorced from reality. In other words, the aim of propaganda 'to destroy the disturbing independence of reality'[74] was most successful on the propagandist himself. How far propaganda was self-destructive in this way is hard to determine, however, since the indeterminant factor is the war. But war, as we have seen above, was inherent in Nazi propaganda from the start, and, as we have also seen, the needs of propaganda themselves hindered the war effort in some areas. The conclusion must be therefore that it contained large self-destructive forces.

NOTES

1. Richard Taylor, 'Goebbels and the Function of Propaganda' in *Nazi Propaganda: the Power and the Limitations*, edited by David Welch (London, 1983), pp. 29–44 (p. 29).
2. Ian Kershaw, 'The Führer Image and Political Integration: The Popular Conception of Hitler in Bavaria during the Third Reich' in *The Führer State: Myth and Reality* (London, 1981), pp. 133–61.
3. Jacques Ellul, *Propaganda* (New York, 1966), p. 284, footnote, and p. 285.
4. Ellul, p. 61.
5. Quoted in Taylor, p. 36.
6. Adolf Hitler, *Mein Kampf* (Boston, 1943). All references, given in brackets in the text, are to this edition.
7. Alan Bullock, *Hitler: a Study in Tyranny* (Harmondsworth, 1962), p. 69.
8. Quoted in Bullock, p. 69.
9. Jeremy Noakes and Geoffrey Pridham, *Documents on Nazism 1919–1945* (London, 1974), p. 340.
10. For example, there is a clear exposition of this idea in Hugh Dalziel Duncan, *Communication and Social Order* (London, 1962), pp. 238–48.

11. Duncan, in a footnote, p. 249, gives Hanfstaengl's account of the origin of this: 'I started playing some of the football marches I had picked up at Harvard. I explained to Hitler all the business about the cheer leaders and college songs and the deliberate whipping up of hysterical enthusiasm. I told him about the thousands of spectators being made to roar, "Harvard, Harvard, Harvard, rah, rah, rah!" in unison and of the hypnotic effect of this sort of thing . . . I had Hitler fairly shouting with enthusiasm. "That is it, Hanfstaengl, that is what we need for the movement, marvelous", and he pranced up and down the room like a drum majorette . . . "Rah, rah, rah!" became "Sieg Heil, Sieg Heil!" – that is the origin of it.'
12. Oron J. Hale, *The Captive Press in the Third Reich* (Princeton, 1964), pp. 31 and 59.
13. Hale, p. 50.
14. Noakes and Pridham, pp. 103–4, and W. S. Allen, *The Nazi Seizure of Power* (New York, 1973), p. 72.
15. Allen, pp. 73–4.
16. Ernest K. Bramsted, *Goebbels and National Socialist Propaganda* (East Lansing, Michigan, 1965), p. 20.
17. Allen, pp. 46–64.
18. Allen, pp. 44 and 135.
19. William L. Shirer, *The Rise and Fall of the Third Reich* (New York, 1960), p. 252.
20. Allen, p. 73.
21. Noakes and Pridham, pp. 108–10, and Allen, pp. 108–9.
22. Bramsted, pp. 23–31.
23. Hamilton T. Burden, *The Nuremberg Party Rallies 1923–1939* (New York, 1967), pp. 38–45.
24. Z. A. B. Zeman, *Nazi Propaganda* (London, 1964), pp. 34–6, and Bullock, pp. 200–1.
25. Some idea of this effect can be gained from Leni Riefenstahl's film, *The Triumph of the Will*, in whose opening sequence shots of clouds, sunlight, and the plane's shadow passing over the columns of men manage to associate the ideas of the eagle and the ancient gods.
26. G. L. Mosse, *Nazi Culture* (New York, 1966), pp. 291–3.
27. Bullock, pp. 217, 230 and 238.
28. Noakes and Pridham, p. 331.
29. Harwood L. Childs, editor, *Propaganda and Dictatorship* (Princeton, 1936), pp. 19–20.
30. Hale, p. 82.
31. Hale, p. 121.
32. Quoted in Hale, p. 155.
33. Hale, p. 267.
34. The editor of the *Völkischer Beobachter* in a 1948 interview, quoted in Hale, p. 246.
35. Hale, p. 323.
36. Hale, p. 232.
37. Walter B. Emery, *National and International Systems of Broadcasting* (East Lansing, Michigan, 1969), pp. 296–8.

38. Bramsted, p. 74.
39. Thomas Grandin, *The Political Use of Radio* (Geneva Studies, vol. 10, No. 3, August 1939), p. 14 and for a detailed account of one such occurrence, Allen, p. 244.
40. Grandin, p. 13.
41. Serge Chakotin, *The Rape of the Masses* (New York, 1940), p. 93.
42. Marshall McLuhan, *Understanding Media: The Extensions of Man* (New York, 1964). In this controversial book, Marshall McLuhan devotes a chapter ('Radio: the Tribal Drum') to radio and makes the claim 'That Hitler came into political existence at all is directly owing to radio and public address systems' (p. 300).
43. Taylor, p. 40.
44. David Welch, *Propaganda and the German Cinema 1933–1945* (Oxford, 1983), p. 311.
45. David Stewart Hull, *Film in the Third Reich* (Berkeley, California, 1969), p. 36.
46. Hull, p. 8.
47. Hull, pp. 118–19.
48. Hull, p. 169.
49. Burden, pp. 97–8.
50. Allen, ch. 14 and, in particular, pp. 225–6.
51. Quoted in Shirer, p. 249.
52. Noakes and Pridham, pp. 353–6.
53. Hull, p. 51.
54. Noakes and Pridham, pp. 358–61.
55. Albert Speer, *Inside the Third Reich* (New York, 1971), pp. 107–8.
56. Quoted in Speer, p. 109.
57. Burden, pp. 60–3.
58. *New York Times*, 12 September 1936, quoted in Burden, p. 128.
59. Quoted in Welch, *Film*, p. 159.
60. *New York Times*, 15 September 1937, quoted in Burden, p. 146.
61. Speer, pp. 45–6.
62. Lothar Kettenacker, 'Sozialpsychologishe Aspekte der Führer Herrschaft' in *The Führer State: Myth and Reality: Politics of the Third Reich* (London, 1981), pp. 98–131, English Summary pp. 131–2 (p. 131).
63. Ellul, p. 121.
64. Ian Kershaw, 'How Effective Was Nazi Propaganda?' in David Welch, *Nazi Propaganda: The Power and the Limitations* (London, 1983), pp. 180–201.
65. Kershaw, 'How Effective', p. 191.
66. Sabina Lietzman, 'Daily Life in the Third Reich', review of *Victims and Neighbors: A Small Town in Nazi Germany Remembered* by Frances Henry, in *The New York Times Book Review* (28 October 1984), p. 38.
67. Siegfried Kracauer, *From Calgari to Hitler: A Psychological History of the German Film* (Princeton, 1947), p. 295.
68. Allen, p. 245.
69. Ellul, pp. 195–7.

70. Joachim Remak, editor, *The Nazi Years* (Englewood Cliffs, New Jersey, 1969), p. 69, for example, but many other examples could be quoted.
71. Norman Stone, *Hitler* (London, 1980), p. 123.
72. Burden, p. 91.
73. Bramsted, pp. 224–7. In the winter of 1942–3 Hitler spoke in public only once, and, after that, there were only two more public speeches and two funeral addresses. From 1943–4 there were only three radio speeches.
74. Kracauer, p. 295.

BIBLIOGRAPHY

Allen, William Sheridan. *The Nazi Seizure of Power.* New York, 1973.

Barsam, Richard Meran. *Filmguide to 'Triumph of the Will'.* Bloomington, Indiana, 1975.

Bessel, Richard. 'Living with the Nazis: Some Recent Writing on the Social History of the Third Reich', review article in *European History Quarterly*, Vol. 14 (1984), pp. 211–20.

Bramsted, Ernest K. *Goebbels and National Socialist Propaganda 1925–1945.* East Lansing, Michigan, 1965.

——. 'The Do's and Don'ts of Goebbels', review of *Politik der Tauschungen* by Fritz Sanger. *The Times Literary Supplement*, 18 June 1976, p. 737.

Bullock, Alan. *Hitler: a Study in Tyranny.* Harmondsworth, 1962.

Burden, Hamilton T. *The Nuremberg Party Rallies 1923–1939.* New York, 1967.

Chakotin, Serge. *The Rape of the Masses.* New York, 1940.

Childs, Harold L., editor. *Propaganda and Dictatorship.* Princeton, 1936.

Doob, Leonard W. 'Goebbels' Principles of Propaganda' in *Public Opinion and Propaganda* by Daniel Katz and others. New York, 1954.

Duncan, Hugh Dalziel. *Communication and Social Order.* London, 1962.

Ellul, Jacques. *Propaganda.* New York, 1966.

Emery, Walter B. *National and International Systems of Broadcasting.* East Lansing, Michigan, 1969.

Gannon, Franklin Reid. *The British Press and Germany.* Oxford, 1971.

German Historical Institute. *The Führer State: Myth and Reality Studies in the Structure and Politics of the Third Reich.* Publications of the German Historical Institute, Vol. 8. London, 1981.

Grandin, Thomas. *The Political Use of Radio.* Geneva Studies, Vol. 10, No. 3, August 1939.

Hale, Oron J. *The Captive Press in the Third Reich.* Princeton, 1964.

Hitler, Adolf. *Mein Kampf.* Boston, 1943.

Hull, David Stewart. *Film in the Third Reich.* Berkeley, California, 1969.

Kracauer, Siegfried. *From Calgari to Hitler: A Psychological History of the German Film.* Princeton, 1947.

Lietzmann, Sabina. 'Daily Life in the Third Reich', review of *Victims and Neighbors: A Small Town in Nazi Germany Remembered* by Frances Henry. *The New York Times Book Review*, 28 October 1984, p. 38.

McLuhan, Marshall. *Understanding Media: The Extensions of Man.* New York, 1964.

Manvell, Roger and Heinrich Fraenkel. *The German Cinema.* New York, 1971.

Mosse, G. L. *Nazi Culture.* New York, 1966.

Noakes, Jeremy, and Geoffrey Pridham. *Documents on Nazism 1919–1945.* London, 1974.

Remak, Joachim, editor. *The Nazi Years*. Englewood Cliffs, New Jersey, 1969.

Shirer, William L. *The Rise and Fall of the Third Reich*. New York, 1960.

Speer, Albert. *Inside the Third Reich*. New York, 1971.

Stone, Norman. *Hitler*. London, 1980.

Trevor-Roper, H. R. *The Last Days of Hitler*. New York, 1947.

Welch, David, editor. *Nazi Propaganda: The Power and the Limitations*. London, 1983.

——. *Propaganda and the German Cinema 1933–1945*. Oxford, 1983.

Zeman, Z. A. B. *Nazi Propaganda*. London, 1964.

Chapter 8

Some errors to avoid

In this final chapter I do not propose to break new ground. The points raised have for the most part been dealt with, at least implicitly, in the preceding chapters. Nevertheless, it is, I feel, valuable to recapitulate the main varieties of error in student papers. My approach is not theoretic, but purely practical. I do not attempt to survey the major danger areas. This chapter is, quite simply, the record of what I have found to be the most frequently committed blunders.

I group my remarks under four heads: Purpose and conclusion; Documentation; Shape and flow; Presentation.

Purpose and conclusion

(a) A research paper should be circular in argument. That is, the formal aim of the paper should be stated in the opening paragraph; the conclusion should return to the opening, and examine the original purpose in the light of the data assembled. It is a prime error to present conclusions that are not directly related to the evidence previously presented. For example, a student paper entitled 'The Significance of Freud' reached, after an examination of Freud's thinking, the following conclusion: 'Because of the application and acceptance of his theories, Sigmund Freud has had a greater influence on both scientific and popular thought and belief than any other psychologist or physician of the past century.' Now this statement may be perfectly true, but as a conclusion it will not stand up. The *title* implies at least a look at Freud's disciples, revisers and opponents. This, in the paper cited, was not performed. The *conclusion* fits the title well enough, but not the body of the paper. The writer was not in a position, on the evidence he had marshalled, to arrive at the conclusion which he did. The student had clearly reverted to the title in making his conclusion without reference to what his paper had actually said.

Now we have to be pragmatic about this. In a strict laboratory sense, it is necessary to lay down *at the start* of the research the aims and methods. The data and conclusions then follow. But in a less rigorously scientific context, one often starts the research with no more than a sense of direction, and pursues it until a pattern emerges. This pattern will then determine the purpose, which is stated at the opening, and this in turn is pursued to the conclusion. The great failure is not to review the work at the end, and not to ensure that the sequence of purpose, data, conclusions forms a consistent and co-ordinated whole.

(b)   A further aspect of purpose should be mentioned. A writer should have a clear idea of the audience to whom the paper is addressed. Is it lay, or specialist? The question is important, because on the answer will turn the inclusion of much subsidiary material. It is easy both to over-emphasize and to under-emphasize the amount of specialized, technical knowledge (and jargon) to be included in a paper. If the subject demands the inclusion of technical terms, a small glossary may be added to the paper. If the subject is of the humanities, but demanding a constant reference to obscure facts, the writer has to consider well how much can be expected of the reader. Even a Professor of History, say, might like to be reminded of the name and office of one of the minor members of Chamberlain's National Government. On the other hand, experts find it extraordinarily irritating to be bombarded with minor information that they are perfectly aware of. The whole question needs to be thought out very carefully. The crime is not to ponder the question: 'For whom am I writing?'

Documentation

(a)   This area I unhesitatingly nominate as having the chief concentration of student failings in the writing of research papers. I need not labour the commoner failings: lack of dates, lack of author's initials, lack of the full details required for documentation. These failings may be ascribed to sloth; as may the simple reluctance to footnote at all. I do not inveigh against sloth; I merely point out that work produced with such disregard for the principle of documentation cannot be dignified with the title of 'Research Paper'. But these are gross crimes. They are worse than crimes: blunders. To claim a large Bibliography (without having made use of it), however, cannot be readily detected, and this must be termed a sin. I can only recommend researchers to set down, in their Bibliographies, no more than may rightfully be claimed. They may be questioned on the sources by their instructors, but essentially the matter remains a private one – between themselves and the Muse of Scholarship.

(b)   As sinful, but more readily detected, is the tendency to pass off a direct quotation as one's own sentence – presumably, to avoid the tedium of appending a footnote. Since sloth is by no means to be correlated with intelligence, it is interesting to observe that writers guilty of this fault quite often carry it out inefficiently. A sudden change of style can be quite easily detected by a perceptive reader. It is not difficult to guess the truth in the following extract: 'What's wrong with advertising? I do not see that the critics have such a good case. It is not clear how far the widespread anxiety and hostility among the intellectual, literary and cultural critics of advertising is shared by the general public. Further, it is not clear how far the fears that advertising inculcates wrong values and habits are supported by evidence.' No great literary gifts are needed to perceive that the first two and last two sentences in this extract are written by different people. The colloquial, decidedly non-literary phrasing of the first part contrasts painfully with the careful, mandarin-type prose of the second. That is why I regard such a practice as unintelligent. Not all styles contrast so obviously; but instructors easily acquire the knack of spotting a word, a phrase, a sentence that is not in key with the rest of the paper. And the effort required to dovetail styles could more easily be directed to inserting quotation marks, and setting down a footnote.

(c)   Even sound and conscientious students, who would not dream of concealing a direct quotation, are sometimes blind to the demands of footnoting. It is *not* sufficient to paraphrase all sources, and write up the paper in one's own words, devoid of footnotes. The Bibliography lists all the sources used, but cannot relate them to the specific points in the paper. Where controversial matters are concerned, it is more than ever important to know *which* authorities are making the point. A paper on the Schlieffen plan, for example, can make a point far more tellingly if it relates this point to Gerhard Ritter, a modern German historian, and does not leave the point to be vaguely associated with an English historian of the 1920s. The whole value of the paper depends on the precise identification of each source used in the argument. One can say, then, that it is a quite basic failing to neglect this identification at all key points.

(d)   A final weakness in this department is the inadequacy of the sources cited. Perhaps three important types of inadequacy may be discerned.

1. First, the sources may be out of date. One may say dogmatically that all Bibliographies should contain several sources published for the first time in the decade before the paper was written. And, however classic their stature, there are few works published before, say, 1970, that do not stand in some need of revision. Such works may be leaned on heavily, but not trusted absolutely. They should be checked against later works, articles and critical reviews. Students should be careful to check the scholarly journals related to their fields, at least for the few preceding years, to ensure that they know of all recent work that has been done in these fields. It is essential to avoid being asked by one's examiner or instructor, 'But were you not aware of the book/article recently published by Professor X?'

However decisive the influence of a seminal work such as Burckhardt's *The Civilization of the Renaissance in Italy* (1860) may be, it is folly to regard it as the epitome of modem thinking on the Renaissance. Even much more recent seminal works stand in some need of being reconsidered. The student should be aware that scholars have invested heavily in change.

2. Second, there is the inadequacy of one-sidedness. This is fatally easy to yield to. Some writers have become influential because they write well; others because they write badly. It is easy to fall under the spell of Macaulay's view of events, because he writes so well. It is easy to accept the ideas of Hegel or Dewey, because they are so hard to read. However they are cast, researchers should coldly resist all spells. They ought to aim at a spread of authorities. Especially they ought to remember that certain subjects are under quite fundamental attacks. They cannot, for example, regard psychoanalysis as a territory owned communally in perpetuity, and

disputed over by Freudians, Adlerians, Stekelites, and so on. They should bear in mind that it is perfectly possible to dismiss psycho-analysis as an aberration in the history of psychology. The root failure in this category is perhaps a superstitious reverence for all manifestations of the printed word.

3. Third, many authorities are simply inadequate in themselves. They are lightweight, unreliable, obviously biased. To this cate-gory belong a variety of articles in the popular press; unsupported and possibly garbled news reports; statements on national policy culled from party political manifestos; puffs and pamphlets; certain works published under the stresses of wartime pressures; works which are openly and blatantly confined to the grinding of a single axe. Such material, the biased and the trivial, may have a useful supporting role to play. No serious paper could be written around it as major sources.

Shape and flow

(a)   The aerodynamic shape, as it were, of the paper I have discussed in Chapter 5. A desirable shape is one in which the *natural form* of the topic has been discerned, and exploited. Failure to do this results in a paper that is as shapely as a sack or an amoeba. I find in practice two main varieties of this deformed shape. In the first variety, the basic structure is sound; but the treatment of a certain part of the paper may be over- or under-done. The bulkiness of a single part of the paper makes the whole work lop-sided; equally, a comparatively skimpy treatment leaves the reader frustrated and dissatisfied. Particularly is this true of topics with a historical basis. The researcher tends in the enthu-siastic early phase to stockpile a mass of notes; the later periods may be less exhaustively treated. The second variety of shape-lessness concerns the inclusion of a side issue. Sometimes the most eager researchers are guilty of this fault. They find them-selves fascinated by an issue worth no more than a brief mention in the paper as a whole; devote considerable pains to covering the issue; and do not have the hardihood to excise this fascinating but irrelevant material. I repeat a warning I have given earlier: much, quite often most, research is *wasted*. One has to bear with this, and be ready to cut. To pursue the anatomical metaphor further, a paper should have a good bone-structure – and a good visual shape.

(b)   On flow, I draw the reader's attention to the remarks on page 68. Absence of flow indicates a stammering, disjointed paper. Apart from the guide words ('however', 'secondly', and so on) which I have recommended, I should like to emphasize the value of headings. A paper which is divided into anonymous 'Sections' and 'Chapters' is much harder to follow than one with descriptive headings. The reader ought to be told exactly what is coming up. Moreover, one can make the mental adjustment far more easily if the eye is helped by spacings, underlinings, use of different coloured inks, and other aids. A little imagination in the exploitation of typographic resources makes a quite amazing difference to the reader's ready comprehension of a paper. Finally, the writer ought if possible to make transitions easy, by referring in the first sentence of a new section to the position arrived at in the previous section.

Presentation

Few, if any, products sell well unless they are seductively packaged. That is a blunt fact of modern life which it is useless to decry, and still more to ignore. A quite astonishing number of students, in my experience, view the matter differently. They are disposed to the view that native worth, untrammelled by conventional presentation, is all. They are apt to regard conventional documentation, format, and even spelling, as in some way a betrayal of their integrity. With this viewpoint I have no desire to undertake a laboured disputation. There are perhaps two points to be made. First, courtesy to one's readers suggests that one make their task as easy as possible. Second, the plainest self-interest demands that one's work be presented in the best possible light. Most of us, I imagine, know the feeling of drafting a passage in longhand – which we think to be not very good – and after typing out the draft, revising our opinion upwards. Essentially the same work looks far better. It is impossible to evade the consequences of this psychological fact. I can see no point whatsoever in neglecting this simple logic: if the world judges by appearances, let the appearances be on one's side.

In practice this has two important implications. Care has to be devoted to the visual techniques of presentation: decent margins, ample spacings, well-judged headings, appropriate underlinings. Then, the final check should be absolute. This is the worst single chore an author has to tackle. There is no escape at all, but I strongly recommend that a friend be induced, on a treaty of reciprocity, to duplicate one's final check. The eye has a quite amazing capacity to miss the identical error a dozen times running. A fresh eye spots it immediately. It is worth the labour. The sense of irritation which a reader experiences when encountering an otherwise excellent work whose appearance is ruined by shoddy presentation is not easily to be described. I have before me a major work, brought out by a reputable publisher, which contains three gross errors on the opening page. It is hard to see the labour of months let down badly for want of half an hour's concentrated checking at the end.

There is one final point to make. The basic virtue of research is accuracy. And for this virtue nobody's memory is sufficient; nobody's care in copying quotations is sufficient. Therefore, let all quotations be checked at the last. I end with the advice of Dr Routh – all wisdom consists of truisms: 'You will find it a very good practice always to verify your references, Sir!'

Chapter 9

Publication in a learned journal

At some point the researcher may wish to publish findings in a learned journal. Characteristically, this will be a matter of preparing a chapter in a thesis or dissertation for publication. The essential guidance and scholarly confirmation have already been provided by the supervisors. It is now up to the researcher. How does one make the transition from academic exercise to published work?

What follows is direct advice. I assume that the reader is in no doubt as to the professional desirability of a wider audience, and of placing a publication on the permanent record. This is how it is done.

1. The first point to grasp is the unsuitability of thesis material in its original form. Editors and publishers loathe theses. That is because they tend to be written in a style too cumbersome for the professional reading public. Theses are written for supervisors who have to be convinced that one has really done the work. No corners are cut. Space is no object. I once remarked to a PhD candidate at his defence of a dissertation on *Macbeth*, 'Enjoy it. This is the last time in your life you will get away with writing 600 pages on a single play.' Nothing of this applies to learned journals. Among other things, editors care about space and foot-notes; they have to cost the printers' bills. They also want to reduce the sawdust factor permissible in theses. The idea that publishing is simply a matter of retyping a thesis chapter, with renumbered pages and a few minor changes, will not long survive in the real world. The material will have to be rethought and rewritten.

2. The professional reading public, for whom the material is reworked, is highly sophisticated. It does not need to have everything spelled out. The writer will have to produce credentials, but need not overwhelm the readers with a parade of footnotes. A culling operation among the lesser footnotes is in order, and the major footnotes ought to imply each other. The professional reading public would like to learn something it did not already know, expressed in succinct prose, the points made in an agile and alert manner. Hence, the writer should think of presenting work that is altogether more *taut* than the original exercise. The fat is shed. What is left is muscle.

3. The great rule is: TARGET THE JOURNAL. It is useless to think, in a general way, of 'preparing work for publication'. That phrase is meaningless. Publication in what? Journals are not interchangeable, and editors are rightly proud of the identity and individuality of their journals. They expect writers to study form for the course, and will give short shrift to those who fail blatantly. They are alert to the novice's error of mailing a paper without regard to the character of the journal. That error guarantees a speedy match of MS to SAE. It is no good thinking vaguely of publishing in sociology, aesthetics, history. The specific journal is everything: *New Statesman and Society*, *History Today*. How does the *British Journal of Aesthetics* rate against the *Journal of Aesthetics and Art Criticism*?

4. Hence, the companion rule is: RESEARCH THE MARKET. The writer should confront the question: How well do you know the available journals in your field? Of course one browses among the open shelves of the library, but unless it is exceptionally well served it can hardly subscribe to all the well-regarded journals in the field. The number of available journals is really enormous. The writer would be well advised to turn back to Chapter 1, Bibliography Section, pages 18–22, where there is general guidance on the various guides to learned journals. In addition, those working in a literary field might like to look at *The Times Literary Supplement* for 22 November 1985, a special issue containing a wide spread of advertisements for literary journals. Language is not necessarily a barrier; certain foreign journals will publish some articles in English. A given article in English might well appear in *Shakespeare Jahrbuch*, or *Cahiers Elisabéthains*, or *Studia Anglia Posnaniensa*.

Then again, research may be of interest to a journal of broader concern than one's own specialist area. Can the material be shaped towards a larger academic or general public? The titles of many well-respected journals give no direct clue as to their contents. North American colleges and universities have a number of excellent journals hospitable to well-written pieces of interest to the general academic community – *Kenyon Review*, *Sewanee Review*, *Virginia Quarterly Review* and so on. There is no quick way of sizing them up. One has to browse through past issues to get an idea of form.

Even in a narrow academic sense, material may be presented from several aspects. Suppose one locates some unpublished letters of G. B. Shaw: the obvious journal is *Shaw Review*. But the letters might bear upon the theatre, upon public life, upon the Fabian Society. Each of these areas implies its own range of interested journals. In the humanities, one should not have hard-and-fast ideas about the 'appropriate' outlet. A certain flexibility and receptivity to new categories is desirable.

5.   One draws up a short list, and then targets the first journal on the list. From now on all efforts are directed to placing an article in that journal. My advice is as follows.

(i)   The selection of the targeted journal precedes the drafting of the paper. Before beginning the draft, immerse yourself in the journal at which you aim. Try to soak up its characteristics. What is its preferred length? Does it favour the blockbuster footnote 1, which sums up all previous research on the subject, or does it prefer a more muted style of documentation? Is your topic well within its range? Should it be cut down, or expanded?

(ii)   If you are in doubt, it is perfectly in order to write a preliminary letter to the Editor, enclosing an abstract of, say, 200 words on the article you have in mind, and asking if it would be welcome. Ideally, the Editor might reply indicating that 2,000 words on the topic would be of interest and would be considered. You then go ahead, working to whatever guidelines have been offered. If the answer is negative, you still have used your time profitably and must now repeat the process with another journal.

(iii) The great principle, for one unused to publication, is that the market speaking through the Editor takes over. Your personal impulses, wishes, idiosyncrasies will have to be restrained. Your prose will in any case be tailored to the house style, if nothing else; your views on the comma in adjectival sequences, for example, will be disregarded. It is the lot of authors.

(iv) The preferred style today is light, dry, crisp. That may not always be apparent in what one reads, but it is the style to aim for. The only advice my first Editor gave me was 'Be concise. Not short, but concise.' That still holds as good advice. The vices are pretentiousness and prolixity. Tone of voice is exceptionally difficult, but must be striven for; the reading public is composed of academic peers. For a general manual of prose style, I warmly recommend F. L. Lucas's *Style* and Sir Ernest Gowers's *Plain Words*. There is still no better crash course in English than George Orwell's essay 'Politics and the English Language'. Always the watchwords are clarity and simplicity.

(v) In presentation, follow the model of an article in the targeted journal, observing its footnote conventions. Do it the way the journal does: if the house style runs to full details of publication (Cambridge: Cambridge University Press, 1982), that is the way you do it. You can retype the notes for a resubmission. The article itself must be submitted on A4 paper with wide margins and double spacing. Read carefully what the Editors say, on the masthead pages, about submission of MSS. If they want SAEs or International Reply Coupons, so be it. Unless stated otherwise, the Editor will expect to receive a clean copy of the MS submitted; you should keep a copy yourself. If the MS is returned in a dog-eared state, retype it, or print out another copy, before the next submission. Editors lost their innocence a long time back, but they still like to receive a MS in pristine condition, that looks as if this is its first outing. Almost invariably the name of the Editor will be known, and stated on the masthead. The covering letter should be addressed to the Editor by name, following the principle that everyone likes to be identified as a human being as well as a functionary. Unless it is desirable to explain some circumstances of the research, it is unnecessary to make a prolonged business of the covering letter. A simple form of words suffices: 'Dear ——, I wish to submit the enclosed article —— to your consideration, for publication in your journal.'

What Editors hope for is quality of research and writing allied to an intelligent and thoughtful attempt to conform to the character of their journals. The successful approach is based on the proposition: this will suit your journal.

Appendix: Some popular Search Engines

Meta-Search Engines

Meta-Search Engines are ones that use several other Search Engines.

Dogpile   *http://www.dogpile.com*

Meta Crawler *http://www.metacrawler.com*

Search Engines

Alta Vista   *http://www.altavista.digital.com*

Ask Jeeves   *http://www.askjeeves.com*

Excite   *http://www.excite.com*

Fast   *http://www.alltheweb.com*

Google   *http://www.google.com*

HotBot   *http://www.hotbot.com*

Infoseek   *http://www.infoseek.com*

Lycos   *http://www.lycos.com*

Webcrawler   *http://www.webcrawler.com*

Yahoo!   *http://www.yahoo.com*

Index